Sex Ethics in the Writings of Moses Maimonides

Sex Ethics in the Writings of Moses Maimonides

Fred Rosner, M.D.

JASON ARONSON INC.
Northvale, New Jersey
London

10 9 8 7 6 5 4 3 2 1

First Jason Aronson Inc. Edition—1994

Library of Congress Cataloging-in-Publication Data

Rosner, Fred.
Sex ethics in the writings of Moses Maimonides / Fred Rosner.
p. cm.
Originally published : New York : Bloch Pub. Co., 1974.
Includes bibliographical references and index.
ISBN 1-56821-323-9
1. Sexual ethics. 2. Sex—Religious aspects—Judaism. 3. Jews—Sexual behavior. 4. Hygiene, Sexual. 5. Maimonides, Moses, 1135-1204. I. Title.
HQ32.R67 1994
296.3′8566—dc20 94-19613

Manufactured in the United States of America. Jason Aronson Inc. offers books and cassettes. For information and catalog write to Jason Aronson Inc., 230 Livingston Street, Northvale, New Jersey 07647.

Dedicated to the memory of
PROFESSOR SUESSMANN MUNTNER
1897–1973
teacher, mentor, colleague and friend

Contents

Preface ix
Introduction 3
Bibliography of Maimonides' Treatise on Cohabitation 11
Maimonides' Treatise on Cohabitation 17
Excerpts on Sex from Maimonides' Other Writings
- Treatise on Hemorrhoids 42
- Treatise on the Regimen of Health 45
- Commentary on the Aphorisms of Hippocrates 49
- Treatise on Asthma 52
- Medical Answers (Responsa) 58
- Mishneh Torah 61
- Medical Aphorisms 66
- Guide for the Perplexed 78
- Book of Holiness 93
- Book of Women 110
- Commentary on the Mishnah 112
- Index 127

Preface

The *Treatise on Cohabitation*, by Moses Maimonides, was written at the request of Al-Malik al Mutsaffar ben Ajjub, Sultan of Hamat, Syria, from 1186 to 1191 A.D. and nephew of Saladin the Great of Egypt. Al-Malik died in 1192, and it thus seems reasonable to assume that this treatise was written in 1190 or 1191, making it one of the earliest, if not the first, medical composition of Maimonides.

In the first of ten chapters, Maimonides describes the reason for writing this treatise—namely, a request by the Sultan who has a desire to increase his sexual potential and coital activities. As in several of his other medical works, Maimonides begins the treatise by showering praises upon the Sultan, whom he addresses as "The Revered Master, may G'd make his glory eternal." The treatise ends with another flowery expression of praise. The substance of the book consists mainly of recipes of foods and drugs which are aphrodisiac in their effect. Also detailed are anaphrodisiac concoctions. Maimonides advises moderation in sexual activity and describes the physiology of sexual temperaments.

There exists an additional longer work with an identical

title, *Treatise on Cohabitation*, which has been erroneously attributed to Maimonides by such renowned scholars as Steinschneider and Kroner (see bibliography). Kroner considers the longer work as the unabridged version of the smaller authentic work. This error was perpetuated until Muntner and Gorlin recently proved the spurious nature of the longer work (see bibliography).

Furthermore, numerous statements on sex and sexual intercourse occur in the other medical writings of Maimonides as well as in his philosophical and theological works. Such pertinent passages are excerpted in the present work. In addition, a new English translation of Maimonides' authentic treatise on cohabitation is presented.

During the preparation of this book, the author learned of the sudden death of his mentor, colleague, co-translator, teacher, collaborator and friend, Professor Suessmann Muntner. The latter met his Creator while walking toward the Western wall *(Kotel Maaravi)* in the Old City of Jerusalem on Sabbath morning, January 20, 1973. The author considers himself fortunate to be counted among the many disciples of Professor Muntner and will forever be indebted to him for all his assistance and helpful advice and criticism over ten years of collaboration in the area of Jewish medical history. In recognition of this long and fruitful association, this book is dedicated to the memory of Professor Suessmann Muntner, 1897–1973.

The author is also indebted to the editors and publishers of the Yale University Press Judaica Series for permission to quote selections from Maimonides' Code, and to Mrs. Sophie Falk for typing the manuscript.

New York FRED ROSNER, M.D.

Sex Ethics in the Writings of Moses Maimonides

Introduction

Moses, son of Maimon (Rambam in Hebrew, Abu Imran Musa Ibn Maimun in Arabic and Maimonides in Greek) was born in Cordova, Spain, on March 30, 1135, which corresponds to Passover eve of the Hebrew year 4895. His ancestry could be traced back to the royal house of King David of Israel. Maimonides' mother died in childbirth and consequently his father *Dayan* (judge) Maimon raised him. Persecution by the Almohades, a fanatical group from North Africa, forced the Maimon family to flee Cordova in the year 1148. Maimonides was thirteen years old. The family wandered through southern Spain and northern Africa for the next ten years and finally settled in Fez, Morocco, in 1158.

Little is known of Maimonides' early life and medical education. It is likely that he studied medicine in Morocco, since in his book of drugs (which we will soon describe), Maimonides refers over one hundred times to medical men of the west and extreme west (i.e., Mohammedan) but only rarely alludes to Spanish or Andalusian physicians. Furthermore, at the end of the book on asthma, Maimonides cites two physicians who were acquaintances of his and who practiced medicine in Fez.

Maimonides must have been an avid reader, since his medical writings show a profound knowledge of Greek and Moslem medical works. Hippocrates, Galen and Aristotle were his Greek medical inspirations and Rhazes of Persia, Al Farabi of Turkey, Ibn Zuhr and Avenzoar are Moslem authors frequently quoted by Maimonides.

The Maimon family left Morocco in 1165, traveled to Palestine, where they landed in Acco, and from there to Egypt, where they settled in Fostat (old Cairo). Maimonides turned to medicine as a livelihood only after the death of his father in 1166 and the death of his brother in a shipwreck shortly thereafter. Maimonides was left with his brother's wife and children to support and, after a year's illness following his father's death, entered into the practice of medicine. In 1174, at age thirty-nine, he was appointed court physician to Vizier Alfadhal, Regent of Egypt during the absence of the Sultan, Saladin the Great, who was fighting in the Crusades in Palestine. It was at this time that Richard the Lion-Hearted, also fighting in the Crusades, is reported to have invited Maimonides to become his personal physician, an offer which Maimonides declined. His reputation as a physician grew in Egypt and neighboring countries, and his fame as theologian and philosopher became worldwide.

In 1193, Saladin died and his eldest son, Al Afdal Nur ad Din Ali, a playboy, succeeded him. As a result, Maimonides' medical duties became even heavier, as described in the famous letter he wrote to his friend, disciple and translator, French Rabbi Samul Ibn Tibbon, in the year 1199:

> . . . I live in Fostat and the Sultan resides in Cairo; these two places are two Sabbath limits [marked-off areas around a town within which it is permitted to move on the Sabbath; approximately one and one half miles] distant from each other. My duties to the Sultan are very heavy. I am obliged to visit him every day, early in the

morning, and when he or any of his children or concubines are indisposed, I cannot leave Cairo but must stay during most of the day in the palace. It also frequently happens that one or two of the officers fall sick and I must attend to their healing. Hence, as a rule, every day, early in the morning I go to Cairo and, even if nothing unusual happens there, I do not return to Fostat until the afternoon. Then I am famished but I find the antechambers filled with people, both Jews and Gentiles, nobles and common people, Judges and policemen, friends and enemies—a mixed multitude who await the time of my return.

I dismount from my animal, wash my hands, go forth to my patients, and entreat them to bear with me while I partake of some light refreshment, the only meal I eat in twenty-four hours. Then I go to attend to my patients and write prescriptions and directions for their ailments. Patients go in and out until nightfall, and sometimes, even as the Torah is my faith, until two hours and more into the night. I converse with them and prescribe for them even while lying down from sheer fatigue. When night falls, I am so exhausted that I can hardly speak.

In consequence of this, no Israelite can converse with me or befriend me (on religious or community matters) except on the Sabbath. On that day, the whole congregation, or at least the majority, comes to me after the morning service, when I instruct them as to their proceedings during the whole week. We study together a little until noon, when they depart. Some of them return and read with me after the afternoon service until evening prayers. In this manner, I spend the days. I have here related to you only a part of what you would see if you were to visit me . . .

Maimonides was also the spiritual leader of the Jewish community of Egypt. At age thirty-three, in the year 1168, shortly after settling in Fostat, he completed his first major work, the *Commentary on the Mishnah*. In 1178, ten years later, his magnum opus, the *Mishneh Torah* was finished. This monumental work is a fourteen-book compilation of all Biblical and Talmudic law and remains a classic to this day. In 1190, Maimonides' great philosophical masterpiece, the *Guide for the Perplexed*, was completed.

Maimonides died on December 13, 1204 (*Tebeth* 20, 4965 in the Hebrew calendar) and was buried in Tiberias. Legend relates that Maimonides' body was placed upon a donkey and the animal set loose. The donkey wandered and wandered and finally stopped in Tiberias. That is the site where the great Maimonides was buried.

Maimonides was a prolific writer. We have already mentioned his famous trilogy, the *Commentary on the Mishnah*, the *Mishneh Torah* and the *Guide for the Perplexed*. Each of these works alone would have indelibly recorded Maimonides' name for posterity. However, in addition to these, he also wrote a *Book on Logic (Ma'amar Hahigayon)*, a Book of Commandments *(Sefer Hamitzvoth)*, an Epistle to Yemen *(Iggereth Hashmad)*, a *Treatise on Resurrection (Ma'amar Techiyath Hamethim)*, Commentaries on several tractates of the Talmud, and over six hundred Responsa. Several additional works including the so-called *Prayer of Maimonides* (1) are attributed to him but are in fact spurious.

Over and above all the books we have just enumerated, Maimonides also wrote ten medical works (2). The first is called *Extracts from Galen*. Galen's medical writings consist of over five hundred books and required two volumes just to catalogue and index them all. Maimonides, therefore, extracted what he considered the most important of Galen's pronouncements and compiled them verbatim in a small work which was intended primarily for the use of students of Greek medicine. This work, as all of Maimonides' medical books, was originally written in Arabic. No complete Arabic manuscript exists today but several Hebrew manuscript translations are available. This work has never been published in any language, but excerpts therefrom in both English and Hebrew appeared recently in a Hebrew periodical (3).

Another medical work of Maimonides is his *Treatise on Poisons and Their Antidotes*. This book is one of the most interesting and popular works because it is very scientific and modern in its approach. It was used as a textbook of toxicology throughout the Middle Ages. The book was written at the request of Maimonides' noble protector, the Grand Vizier and Supreme Judge Al Fadhil, who in 1199 asked Maimonides to write a treatise on poisons for the layman which could guide him before the arrival of a physician. In the introduction, Maimonides praises Al Fadhil and his feats in war and peace. He mentions Al Fadhil's orders to import from distant lands ingredients lacking in Egypt but necessary for the preparation of two antidotes against poisonings, the Great Theriac and the Electuary of Mithridates.

The first section of the book deals with snake bites, dog bites, and scorpion, bee, wasp and spider stings. The first chapter concerns the conduct of the victim in general. Thus Maimonides states as follows:

> When someone is bitten, immediate care should be taken to tie the spot above the wound as fast as possible to prevent the poison from spreading throughout the body; in the meantime, another person should make cuts with a black lancet directly above the wound, suck vigorously with his mouth and spit out. Before doing that, it is advisable to disinfect the mouth with olive oil, or with

> spirit in oil . . . Care should be taken that the sucking person has no wound in his mouth, or rotten teeth . . . should there be no man available to do the sucking, cupping-glasses should be applied, with or without fire; the heated ones have a much better effect because they combine the advantages of sucking and cauterizing at the same time . . . Then apply the great theriac . . . Apply to the wound some medicine which should draw the poison out of the body.

In his book on poisons, Maimonides also describes the long incubation period for rabies (up to 40 days). Numerous Arabic, Hebrew and Latin manuscripts are extant (4). A German translation was published in 1873 by Steinschneider (5). A French translation appeared in 1865 by Rabbinowicz and was reprinted in 1935 (6). An English translation of Steinschneider's German version is that of Bragman in 1926 (7). The definitive Hebrew edition of Muntner appeared in 1942 (8), and Muntner's English version was published in 1966 (9).

Another authentic medical book of Maimonides is the *Glossary of Drug Names.* This work was discovered very recently by Max Meyerhof, an Egyptian ophthalmologist, in the Aya Sofia library in Istanbul, Turkey, as Arabic manuscript No. 3711. Dr. Meyerhof edited the original Arabic and provided a French translation, which he published in 1940 in Cairo (10). A Hebrew edition by Muntner appeared in 1969 (11) and an English translation by Rosner and Muntner is in preparation. The work is essentially a pharmacopoeia and consists of 405 short paragraphs containing names of drugs in Arabic, Greek, Syrian, Persian, Berber and Spanish.

The other medical writings of Maimonides are briefly described later in this book where excerpts on sexual intercourse are quoted.

Maimonides' medical writings are varied, comprising extracts from Greek medicine, a series of monographs on health in general and several diseases in particular, and a recently discovered pharmacopoeia demonstrating Maimonides' extensive knowledge of Arabic medical literature and his familiarity with several languages. Some people feel that Maimonides' medical writings are not as original as his theological and philosophical writings. However, his medical works demonstrate the same lucidity, conciseness and formidable powers of systematization and organization so characteristic of all his writings. The *Book on Poisons*, the *Regimen of Health*, and the *Medical Aphorisms of Maimonides* became classics in their fields in medieval times.

The following paragraph was written in an early paper on Maimonides (12):

> Maimonides died on December 13, 1204 (*Tebet* 20, 4965, in the Jewish Calendar), and was buried in Tiberias, Palestine, at his own request. The Christian, Moslem and Jewish worlds mourned him. His literary ability was incredible and his knowledge encyclopedic. He mastered nearly everything known in the fields of theology, mathematics, law, philosophy, astronomy, ethics, and, of course, medicine. As a physician, he treated disease by scientific method, not by guesswork, superstition, or rule of thumb. His attitude towards the practice of medicine came from his deep religious background, which made the preservation of health and life a divine commandment. His inspiration lives on through the years and his position as one of the medical giants of history is indelibly recorded. He was physician to sultans and princes, and as Sir William Osler said, "He was Prince of Physicians." The heritage of his great medical writings is being more and more appreciated. To the Jewish people he symbolized the highest spiritual and

intellectual achievements of man on this earth; as so aptly stated, "from Moses to Moses there never arose a man like Moses," and none has since.

1. Rosner, F., "The Physician's Prayer Attributed to Maimonides," *Bull. Hist. Med.*, 41, 1967, pp. 440–454.
2. Rosner, F., "Maimonides, the Physician: A Bibliography," *Bull. Hist. Med.*, 43, 1969, pp. 221–235.
3. Barzel, V., "The Art of Cure: A Non-Published Medical Book by Maimonides," *Harofe Haivri*, 2 1955, pp. 82–83 (Hebr.) and 177–185 (Eng.).
4. Rosner, F., "Moses Maimonides' Treatise on Poisons," *J.A.M.A.*, 205, 1968, pp. 94–916.
5. Steinschneider, M., "Gifte und ihre Heilung," *Virchows Arch. F. Path. Anat.*, 57, 1873, pp. 62–120.
6. Rabbinowicz, I.M., *Traité des poisons.* Paris: Lipschutz, 1935. 70 pp. (1st ed. 1865)
7. Bragman, L.J.; "Maimonides' Treatise on Poisons," *Med. J. and Rec.*, 124, 1926, pp. 103–107.
8. Muntner, S., *Moshe ben Maimon (Maimonides), Samei hamaveth veharafuoth kenegdam* (Poisons and their antidotes, or "The treatise to the honored one"). Jerusalem: Rubin Mass, 1942. XX and 233 pp. (Hebr.).
9. Muntner, S., *Treatise on Poisons and Their Antidotes. The Medical Writings of Moses Maimonides*, Vol. 2. Philadelphia: Lippincott, 1966. XXXVII and 77 pp.
10. Meyerhof, J., *Un glossaire de matière médicale, composé par Maimonide (Sarh Asma al'Uqqa)*, Mém. Inst. Egypte, Vol. 41. LXXVI and 256 pp.
11. Muntner, S., *Moshe ben Maimon. Biyur Shaymoth Harefuoth. (Lexicography of Drugs and Medical Responses).* Jerusalem: Mossad Harav Kook, 1969. 164 pp.
12. Rosner, F., "Moses Maimonides (1135–1204)," *Ann. Int. Med.*, 62, 1965, 372–375.

Bibliography of Maimonides' Treatise on Cohabitation

Moses Maimonides' *Treatise on Cohabitation (Fi-al Jima* in Arabic; *Ma'amar Hamishgal* in Hebrew; *De Coitu* in Latin) is extant in an Arabic manuscript (Sacre Monte #111[2]) with Hebrew letters in Granada, Spain (1–7). A fragment exists also in the Bodleian Library in Oxford as Arabic Manuscript Uri 608. Another fragment in Hebrew letters was found by Muntner in Paris Manuscript #1211 but is incorrectly bound at folios 96, 98, 99 and 101.

This treatise was twice translated into Hebrew, once by Rabbi Zerachiah ben Itzchak ben Shealtiel Chen in Rome in approximately 1277, and once by an unknown translator.

Rabbi Zerachiah's Hebrew translation entitled *Maamar al Ribooy Hatashmish* is extant in several manuscripts:

a) Munich #111[4]
b) Paris #335 (the translator's name is distorted to Zachariah)
c) Parma De Rossi #150 (under the misleading name *De Cibo et Alimentu*)

The anonymous Hebrew translation entitled *Maamar Hamishgal* is also extant in numerous manuscripts:

a) Bodleian, Oxford #72[6]
b) Paris #1120[4] (concludes with a recipe by Maimonides' son)
c) Paris #1173 (concludes with a recipe by Maimonides' son)
d) Parma De Rossi #1280
e) Vienna #153 (p. 164, Gold.; .87)
f) Rabinowitz #1886 n. 43
g) Steinschneider # 30 f. 96–98 incomplete (later Berlin #232. Qu.836[5])
h) Berlin #72 (Qu. 545[6])
i) two manuscripts in the Jewish Theological Seminary that are identical to Paris #1173 (item c above)

A Latin translation was made by the apostate John De Capua. Steinschneider (2) is not certain whether the Latin translation was made from the Hebrew or from the Arabic, but Kroner (4) states with assurance that the Latin version stemmed from the Hebrew. Muntner (7) also feels that De Capua used Zerachiah's Hebrew version. The Latin manuscripts extant today (1, 7, 8) are:

1) Vienna Tab II, 47 #2280[4] (*De Coitu*)
2) Venice St. Marc. Valentinelli V. Cod 26[14] *(Regimen Coadjuvans ad coitum)*
3) Ms Friedenwald ff 29V-31. *(De Coitu: Dixit Moyses filius servi dei ysraelita cordubensis mandavit dominus meus . . . Dominus autem eligat sibi ex hiis que facilia sunt, et quandoque utatur hoc, quandoque illo; cuius gloriam deus conseruet in secula. Amen)*

Muntner (7) mentions another Latin manuscript which is probably identical with that of Friedenwald.

The first critical edition of Maimonides' *Treatise on Cohabitation* was prepared by Kroner in 1906 (4). Kroner edited and published the Parma and Munich Hebrew manuscripts, together with a German translation of the Munich manuscript. In addition, Kroner published his edited rendition of a totally different and much longer work, Munich Arabic manuscript #877, II, which he thought represented another treatise by Maimonides on sexual intercourse, probably the unabridged version of the shorter work.

Steinschneider, who himself had wished to edit and publish the various manuscripts of Maimonides' *Treatise on Cohabitation* (1, 2) also feels that Munich Arabic manuscript #877, II, is a longer version of the authentic shorter work by Maimonides on coitus. This longer version consists of 19 chapters, whereas all the Hebrew and Latin manuscripts are only 10 chapters long.

After much study and evaluation of both these works on sexual intercourse, Muntner (7) and Gorlin (6) concluded that the longer version is spurious and was not written by Maimonides. The reasons are as follows:

a) no Hebrew or Latin translation of the longer 19-chapter work exists. All of Maimonides' authentic works have both Hebrew and Latin manuscript versions extant, except the *Extracts from Galen.*
b) the style and introduction are different from other writings of Maimonides.
c) the longer work includes numerous references to nonrational therapeutics which are not in keeping with the totally rational approach to medicine that Maimonides uses in his other medical writings.
d) no ancient medical authorities are quoted in the longer version. In all of Maimonides' other medical writings, Greek and Arabic physicians are quoted. In the shorter authentic version of Maimonides' treatise on coitus, Avicenna and Avenzoar are cited.
e) the longer version is not an unabridged version of the shorter one. The contents are quite dissimilar.
f) the longer work is not bound with any other of Maimonides' medical writings.
g) Rabbi Meir Aldabi of Spain, grandson of the re-

nowned Talmudic codifier, Rabbi Asher ben Yechiel, in his famous book *Sheviley Emunah,* written in 1360, quotes only the Hebrew translation (9), although he was fluent in Arabic. It seems likely that only the shorter version of the treatise on sex was recognized by Aldabi as having been authored by Maimonides.

In 1916 Kroner edited and published the original Arabic text (5) from the only extant Arabic manuscript (Granada, Sacre Monte #111²) of the authentic version of Maimonides' treatise on sex. A critique of Kroner's effort was published by Seidel in 1918 (10). Both Kroner (4, 5) and Steinschneider (1, 2) remained without doubt that both short and long versions of the work on coitus are authentic and written by Maimonides. However, the arguments that Muntner (7) and Gorlin (6) present, as enumerated above, are not easily refuted.

English translations of both authentic and spurious versions of Maimonides' *Treatise on Cohabitation* were published by Gorlin in 1961 (6). Gorlin's English version of the authentic work is based mainly on Kroner's German translation. Gorlin's work, without mention of his name, was translated anonymously into Spanish (11). An Italian translation of the authentic and spurious works based on Kroner's 1906 editions of both (4) appeared in 1960 (12), with introductions and commentary by Umberto de Martini of Rome.

A Hebrew edition of the authentic work was published in 1965 by Muntner (7) and a Hebrew translation of the spurious work, also by Muntner, appeared in 1965 (13).

The present work represents an English translation of the Zerachiah ben Shealtiel Chen Hebrew version of Maimonides' authentic *Treatise on Cohabitation.* The only heretofore available English rendition of this work (6) is deficient in many respects as the translator Gorlin himself points out (14): ". . . some of the translations given have not been literal but paraphrased and excerpted . . . a considerable amount of errors have probably crept into this work . . ."

I thus felt the need for a more precise and accurate translation of this important medieval medical treatise of Maimonides. The present translation is based on several Hebrew manuscripts, particularly Paris Ms #1120, Munich Ms #111 and Parma Ms #1280. In addition, the original Arabic manuscript Sacre Monte #111[2] from Granada as well as Kroner's German (4, 5) and Muntner's Hebrew (7) editions were consulted. Words in parentheses are my own additions, not present in the original but necessary to clarify the meaning of certain words or phrases. Minor differences in the various manuscript versions are indicated in the notes.

1) Steinschneider, M., *Die Hebräischen Übersetzungen des Mittelalters und die Juden als Dolmetscher. Ein Beitrag zur Literaturgeschichte des Mittelalters, meist nach handschriftlichen Quellen.* Berlin, 1893, pp. 763–764.
2) Steinschneider, M., *Die Arabische Literatur der Juden. Ein Beitrag zur Literaturgeschichte der Araber, Grossenteils aus Handschriftlichen Quellen.* Frankfurt A.M.: J. Kauffmann, 1902, p. 213.
3) Brockelmann, C., *Geschichte der Arabischen Literatur. Zweite den Supplementbanden angepasste Auflage.* Erster Band. Leiden: E. J. Brill, 1943, p. 646.
4) Kroner, H., *Ein Beitrag zur Geschichte der Medizin des XII Jahrhunderts an der Hand zweier medizinischer Abhandlungen des Maimonides auf Grund von 6 unedierten Handschriften. Dargestellt und kritisch beleuchtet.* Itskowski Oberforf-Bopfingen, 1906, p. 116 (Ger.) and p. 28 (Hebr.).
5) Kroner, H., *"Eine Medizinische Maimonides Handschrift aus Granada. Ein Beitrag zur Stilistik des Maimonides und zur Characteristik der Hebräischen Übersetzungsliteratur. Im Urtext herausgegeben, ubersetzt und kritisch erläutert," Janus* 21, 1916, pp. 203–247.
6) Gorlin, M., Maimonides' "On Sexual Intercourse." *Fi'L-Jima.* Translated from the Arabic with an Introduction and Commentary. Brooklyn: Rambash Publishing Co., 1961. 128 pp.
7) Muntner, S., *Rabbenu Moshe Ben Maimon. Ma'amar Al Chizuk Ko'ach Hagavra* (On the Increase of Sexual Vigor). Translated by Rabbi Zerachiah Ben Shealtiel Chen. Jerusalem: Mos-

sad Harav Kook, 1965, pp. 33–66. (Bound together with Maimonides' treatises on hemorrhoids and asthma.)

8) Friedenwald, H., *Jewish Luminaries in Medical History.* Baltimore: Johns Hopkins Press, 1946, p. 99.

9) Aldabi, M., *Sheviley Emunah* (Paths of Faith), Section V, Chapter 8, 1360.

10) Seidel, E., *Kroner (Rabbiner). Eine Medizinische Maimonides Handschrift aus Granada. Beitrag zur Stilistik des Maimonides und zur Charakteristik der Hebräischen Übersetzungsliteratur. Im Urtext herausgegeben Übersetzt und kritisch erläutert. Janus, Jahrgang* XXI, S. 203–247. *Mitteilungen zur Geschichte der Medizin und der Naturwissenschaften.* Leipzig, 1918, v. 17, pp. 49–54.

11) *"Notas Introductorias Al 'Guia Sobre El Contacto Sexual' de Maimonides," Anales de Ars Medici-Mexico,* Vol. 5, No. 4, July 1961, pp. 240–248.

12) De Martini, U., *Maimonide Segreto dei Segreti.* Roma: A Cura dell'Istituto di Storia della Medicina dell' Universita di Roma, 1960. 84 pp.

13) Muntner, S., *"Ma'amar al Razey Hachajim Haminiyim Meyuchas Le Rabbenu Moshe Ben Maimon"* (Pseudo-Maimonides, On Sexual Life), in *Al Hachayim Haminiyim.* Geniza, Jerusalem, 1965, pp. VIII and 108.

14) reference 6, p. 22.

Maimonides' Treatise on Cohabitation

Chapter 1

Thus speaks Moses, the son of the Lord's Servant, the Israelite from Cordova:[1] the Revered Master, may G'd make his glory eternal, has commanded me to instruct him in a regimen that is helpful in increasing sexual potential,[2] because he said that he has a weakness in this regard, coupled with this Servant's[3] observing leanness of the Master's body and diminution of his flesh to the point that he approaches emaciation. In addition, his (natural) constitution tends somewhat toward heat.[4] He mentioned to me—may his glory increase—that he would not abandon any part of his sexual activities. Indeed, he wishes this regimen because of fear, due to the meagerness of his body. He desires these increases (in coital activities) because of the multitude of young maidens. He further requests—may the Lord make his glory eternal—that I only mention in this regimen that which is easy to carry out and whose performance is pleasant.

And the Servant (Maimonides) looked into the matter that was impressed upon him and saw (appropriate) to select[5] medications and foods which are beneficial for this, which are abundant,[6] whose consumption is customary in this country, and which do not predominantly heat (the body), since this was mentioned as the condition of his (natural) constitution. The Servant saw (appropriate) to present[7] a comprehensive treatise (on this subject) and it is as follows:

It is well known to physicians that nutriments for this purpose are of much greater value than medications,[8] since, in reality,[9] sperm is a superfluity of food which remains from that which the organs require during the third digestion.[10] The body weakens if one indulges excessively therein together with the damage that occurs from the exertion of coitus.[11]

Chapter 2

And know that all the (foods or medications) that cool the body or the organs of coitus, as well as all that which dries the body or these same organs, are extremely detrimental. Among foods, medications, and other regimens (of health), all that which moistens and warms to an intermediate degree is extremely beneficial to the entire body or to the organs of coitus in this regard.[12] For example, happiness, delight, laughter,[13] rest, and sleep[14] that is not excessive are of value in this matter.[12] And the opposite of these is extremely detrimental: that is mourning,[15] sorrow, anxiety, fasting, weariness, toil and wakefulness[14]—all these markedly abolish erection and diminish the sperm.[16] And similarly, excessive mention of the subject of intercourse, and discussions thereof, and praising it, are among the things that are helpful (for coitus), whereas directing one's thoughts far therefrom causes the penis to shrink and weakens its activity.

In addition, the engagement in coitus for lust[17] is among the things that strengthen the penis and aid in increasing sexual intercourse, whereas engagement therein without lust weakens the penis, causes it to shrivel up and diminishes the desire (for coitus). All the more so if one combines with this the elimination[18] of thoughts (of intercourse) and the abstention from the act itself, since this is the first thing that the abstainers[19] practice to save themselves from licentiousness.[20]

Chapter 3

And it is known that this activity[21] is not purely a natural function;[22] that is, erection is not similar to nutritional or growth activities[22a] in which emotions[23] play no part. Rather it is also an emotional process controlled by the psyche.[23] As a result, various emotions[24] can be greatly detrimental or beneficial (for coitus): i.e., sorrow, anxiety and mourning,[15] or the repulsiveness of the woman with whom one intends to have sexual intercourse, are among the things that markedly weaken coitus. The converse emotions incite one thereto and produce a powerful stimulation.[25]

Physicians have already mentioned that which especially weakens coitus: sexual intercourse with numerous maidens, elderly women, or a young girl that has not reached puberty, or a woman who for many years has not been intimate, or a menstruating[26] or ill woman; even more than all this is coitus with a repugnant woman who has passed the menopause[27] and is repulsive for this reason.[28] Indeed, nature teaches and accustoms one to laziness[29] if (a woman's condition) has converted to this (post-menopausal) state. Therefore, whenever a person has the desire (for coitus) but finds his lust insufficient, he should follow the regimen that can be gleaned from this, my treatise, which includes that which should be striven for, and that which should be avoided in this regard.

Chapter 4

I will now commence to enumerate various details which fall under the fundamental principle that I mentioned first: (sexual potency is increased by) all that which gives rise to good and beneficial[30] blood, and all that which warms and moistens the body, and which contains gas that dissolves in the third digestion.

The following are the foods which are of value for this (purpose): the meat of lambs[31] and pigeons,[32] and all brains, especially the brains of chickens. And doves and birds and rooster testicles[33] are extremely beneficial in increasing sperm and its production for (people of) all temperaments and all ages. Similarly (of benefit to increase sexual potential are) bone marrow[34] and the yolk of chicken eggs,[35] and the eggs of doves, and the eggs of the partridge,[36] and birds' eggs[37] and fresh milk as it issues forth from the nipples.[38]

Among (aphrodisiac) plants are the turnip,[39] lettuce,[40] onions, especially the white varieties,[41] the fennel,[42] mint which is mentha,[43] peas,[44] beans,[45] the lubiya,[46] sesame[47] and asparagus.[48]

Among the fruits of trees: peeled dried almonds,[49] hazelnuts,[50] grapes, pistachio,[52] and indican nuts,[53] as well as kernels of *Alazel* meaning *Al Zalna*[54] which is known as black pepper,[55] are all nutriments that have been found to be advantageous for this matter (of coitus) and they aid erection. Among them are those which, if taken singly or in combination, depending upon the compounding thereof, increase the sperm.

And the imbibition of honey water helps erection.[55a] And of greater benefit than any food or medicine[56] for the aforementioned matter is wine. There is no substitute for it in this respect[57] because the blood that is produced therefrom is warm and moist and rejoices the soul,[58] and strongly incites to sexual intercourse because of its special characteristic[59] which is linked to nature and fills the (blood) vessels with much good vapor. This is the movement of erection.[60] This is especially so if one takes some (wine) with craving,[61] and after the meal, and when one leaves the bath, for its effect in this regard is far greater than anything else.

Chapter 5

And know that seeds which warm and dry (the body also) dry the sperm and weaken coitus, especially those (seeds) which have the capacity to produce winds[62] such as juice from rue,[63] caraway,[64] black caraway,[65] general caraway,[66] pepper[67] and mustard.[68] For this reason, it is proper to avoid all seeds and condiments with which foods are seasoned except those which I will enumerate and these are the following: one ounce each of long pepper[69] and galanga,[70] two ounces each[71] of cinnamon[72] and anise,[73] and one quarter ounce each of mace[74] and muscat nut. These medications should be pulverized and thus ready to season any food that is to be cooked. The powder (of these spices) should be sprinkled over the food. One should utilize of these as much as is advantageous.[75]

Indeed, the foods and medications that one should avoid are all those which cool or dry (the body) or produce flatulence. Among the items we are accustomed to are lentils,[76] gilban[77] and cooling vegetables,[78] such as wormwood[79] and spinach.[80] Even more so is lettuce,[81] since it is strongly detrimental in this regard. In addition, cucumbers[82] and melons[83] and (other) sour substances are all extremely harmful (for coitus), and the worst (offender of all) is vinegar.

I have already mentioned that one should avoid all seeds except those that I have enumerated. Similarly, turnip[84] seeds produce headaches and dry the sperm. Among the things we are accustomed to that one should strongly avoid is nilophar,[85] because its particular attribute is to destroy sperm, and it is as if it counteracts (coital potential) so that even its aroma weakens sexual intercourse, because of this attribute within it.

Chapter 6

And it is appropriate that I mention compounded medications and combinations of foods[86] which are (beneficial) for this matter (of coitus). I will commence with foods: (one such dish is) prepared from meat of one-year-old[87] sheep, and peas,[88] and carrots,[89] and turnips, and white onions, and yolks of chicken eggs, and the condiments that we have mentioned,[90] so that their flavor be savory.[91]

Another (food preparation) is made from the meat of a lamb, or castrated rooster,[92] or pigeons,[93] with cow's milk, and (all) this should be seasoned with the seeds we have described.[94]

Harissiya[95] is made with the meat of a lamb[96] or a castrated rooster,[97] and seasoned with the seeds we have mentioned. Then one should add cinnamon powder thereto. If one drinks warm milk in the quantity of one liter, and if one sprinkles thereon one quarter *mishkal*[98] of ground and sifted carnation,[99] then this remedy is extremely beneficial and provides (more frequent and/or more powerful) erections and increases the sperm. In addition, roasted onions are very valuable, because of their (aphrodisiac) property, and one should not withhold sprinkling thereon the powder of the seeds we have mentioned.[94] (Physicians) have stated that roasted onion, together with boiled egg yolk, produces an excellent result. Similarly, if one sprinkles some of the aforementioned spices on the yolk of a soft-boiled egg, (one produces a good aphrodisiac). One should consume approximately ten (portions[100]) thereof before retiring, and this stimulates (desire for) sexual intercourse and increases the sperm.

Avicenna has mentioned a cake with the following composition which strengthens sexual intercourse,[101] and the following is its preparation: take the sum of fifty brains of birds[102] and doves, and twenty yolks of bird's[102] eggs, and ten yolks of spring-chicken eggs, and one portion of the juice of pounded and crushed lamb's meat, and three ounces of the juice of roasted onions, and five ounces of carrot juice,[103] and the necessary quantity of salt and spicy seasonings, and fifty drachms of butter. From (all) this, prepare a cake and eat it and, after its digestion, drink strong wine which has a good aroma and which tends towards sweetness.

And behold, derived from this treatise of his,[104] I have composed a cake which is easy to prepare and has a pleasant taste. The one for whom I composed it told me that he found a great (aphrodisiac) effect therein.

Its preparation[105] (is as follows): take four onions and roast them in the oven until they are done,[106] and remove their outer peel and grind them up well. In addition, take one half liter of boiled lamb's meat and roast it in its own gravy until it is completely done. Grind the meat and combine it with the roasted onions, together with the remaining broth. Upon this place twenty yolks of chicken eggs, and mix everything together. Add to this that quantity of the aforementioned spices which makes the flavor savory.[91] (Also add) a little salt, and if the salt is from the skink,[107] this is preferable. Roast it in sesame oil,[108] or in butter. And one can also prepare it just as this cake itself (but) with boiled and fried carrots substituted for the onions. One can also prepare it with both onions and carrots as I have described.

Another (aphrodisiac) cake (is made as follows): take three ounces of rooster testicles,[109] and three ounces of birds' brains,[110] and twenty yolks of chicken eggs—should you use dove eggs, this is much preferable—and the aforementioned spices. Roast them in sesame oil or in butter. One can also prepare (this cake) with brains of lambs[111] instead of the meat, and this has a good (aphrodisiac) effect.

Chapter 7

Avicenna—and apart from him other physicians—mentions (various) types of beneficial sweet substances. Behold, from among them we have made known a sweet substance which is easy to prepare, has a pleasant taste, and has been tested (and found effective).

Its preparation (is as follows: take) two ounces each of pine kernels,[112] pistachio kernels,[113] and almond kernels,[114] one ounce each of fried sesame (which is gulgulan),[115] eruca seeds,[116] and seed kernels of the melon; and four liters of sugar and bee's honey whose foam was removed. The kernels are all roasted in sesame oil until it congeals, and thus is prepared the conventional sweet (aphrodisiac) substance. And the fire should not be too strong.

Another sweet (aphrodisiac) substance is (prepared) by soaking peas, and one should soak them in eruca water until they split and peel. Take one portion thereof and a portion of each of the aforementioned kernels, and roast all this in sesame oil until it congeals, as is usual with a sweet substance.[117]

Let my Lord Master know that these foods, prepared (specifically to increase) sexual intercourse, should be consumed after leaving the bath. If it is possible that one drink the measure of three ounces of aromatic wine thereafter, then this is better for the intended (purpose of coitus), as well as for fattening the (Sultan's emaciated) body.

Chapter 8

Among compounded (aphrodisiac) medications there is included electuary of carrots[118] or *saqaqil,*[119] and their action[120] is one and the same, because *saqaqil* is the wild carrot.

Their preparation (is as follows): take the outer[121] portion of the carrots or *saqaqil,* discard that which is inside and boil them and cool them a little, and squeeze them with your hand. Take one liter of either of them,[122] three ounces each of eruca seed, peeled sesame which is peeled gulgulan,[115] bird's tongue[123] and pine kernels, three liters of honey whose foam was removed, and prepare all this in the manner that all electuaries are prepared. Afterwards take three drachms each of red behen[124] (which is *Bi'am Ro'bi* in Arabic), and white behen[125] (which is album), and galanga,[126] and long pepper;[127] and four drachms each of cinnamon[128] and doronic.[129] Improve its aroma (by adding one) *mishkal* of myrrh[130] oil, and consume one mouthful thereof daily, because it will provide a recognizably good (aphrodisiac) effect. It is approximately equal in effectiveness to the scincus, which is the sheit fish.[131]

Another (aphrodisiac) remedy: take a liter of milk, dissolve forty drachms of manna[132] therein, and cook until it thickens. Consume the amount of one third liter daily. This is how physicians mention it. However, I have combined one quarter drachm of carnation[133] with this to increase its effectiveness.

Another remedy (is made as follows: take one drachm each[134] of asparagus seed[135] (which is *Halyun* in Arabic), Solomon's tooth (which is *saqaqil*)[136], and ginger;[137] three drachms each of white and red behen,[138] and roasted marine onion,[139] and navel[140] of the sheit fish;[131] two drachms each of lucerne seeds[141] (which is said to be favil, and others say it is reed seeds), eruca seeds, bird's tongue,[123] urtica seeds[142] and radish seeds,[143] and forty[144] drachms of sugar and four drachms of cinnamon.[145]

Among the beneficial medicaments (for coitus, physicians) mention an electuary of grains. (It is prepared as follows): one portion each of almonds, hazelnuts, peeled and scraped pistachio and indican nuts,[146] pines,[147] seeds of the *alkalkal*[148] which is that which is sold[148a] as a substitute for balsam seeds,[149] *alzalem*[150] grains which are black peppers, terebinth[151] seeds, and twenty portions[151a] each of long pepper and ginger. All this is pulverized and kneaded into a *panid*,[152] and one consumes thereof daily as much as an egg.

A syrup which they say increases the lust for coitus and increases the sperm (is the following): take *silgam*[153] (which is turnips)[154] and figs[155] and these should be well-cooked[156] and strained.[157] Upon this sprinkle panise and place it upon the fire until it boils and is converted to wine.[158] The patient imbibes it and becomes lustful (for sexual intercourse).

They[159] have already mentioned (the following) as being especially efficacious for this purpose: take the maleness[160] of an ox,[161] pulverize it, and sprinkle the powder on a soft-boiled egg and eat it.

They also state[162] that *alskanker*[163] meat is famous and well known (as an aphrodisiac), and in particular its navel[164] as well as its salt with which its abdomen[165] is salted. One should immerse (food) in this salt and cook the food therein, and this will greatly strengthen it.[166]

They state that so too is the date palm,[167] which is also (an aphrodisiac), in that its meat has a most excellent effect indeed.

And Ibn Zohr[168] has mentioned the following medication, and stated that it is a beneficial electuary for deficient erections and diminution in sperm and desire (for coitus: take) one portion each of testicles of the *al falid* fox,[169] ginger, long pepper, turnip seed, and garden radish seed, one portion each of ox-tongue blossom,[170] giant fennel,[171] and eruca, and one third of a portion of the sheit fish.[172] Grind them separately and sieve that which should be sieved, and knead (all this) with apple juice,[173] and eat between three and four drachms thereof.

Chapter 9

They[174] also state that because there are many people who desire to have prolonged erection and who are unable to ejaculate,[175] it seems appropriate that I mention the following remedy. It is a wondrous secret which no person has (heretofore) described: take one liter each of carrot oil, and radish oil, one quarter liter of mustard oil, combine it all and place therein one half liter of live saffron-colored ants. Set the oil in the sun for between four and seven days and afterwards utilize it. Massage the penis[176] therewith for three hours or two hours before sexual intercourse. Then wash it with warm water, and it will remain in erection even after ejaculation. Nothing comparable has yet been prepared for this purpose.

Another (aphrodisiac) which he mentions besides[177] (the aforementioned one consists of the following): one drachm of pyrethrum,[178] one half drachm of euphorbia,[179] and one quarter drachm of musk.[180] All this is pulverized and diluted in an ounce of jasmine oil,[181] and one massages therewith daily near the genitals and the testicles and the penis.[182]

Chapter 10

Verily, the regimen which one should follow in regard to choosing one of these foods or medicaments[183] is to enter the bath once every five days but not to tarry there long. And one should smell the aroma of warming substances, such as myrrh[184] and amber[185] and galia.[186] And one should eat after the bath and, if possible, drink pleasant-smelling wine or a honey electuary. And one should massage one's feet every night before retiring until they redden, after having washed them in warm water. One should do this in summer and winter, because whenever the feet become cold,[187] erection subsides and diminishes. Similarly, one should strive to constantly warm the depth of the abdomen,[188] and anoint it with much butter.[189] This is the goal[190] which I intended (to convey) regarding this (aphrodisiac) regimen.

That which we have found to be best for this purpose is to massage the entire depth of the abdomen[188] upon awakening from one's sleep with a thick, hairy cloth which should be hot, together with something that warms.[191] Following this one massages it[192] strongly with the palm of one's hand, using oil which has a pleasant aroma. It should contain some myrrh[193] with which one also massages, because the latter is more specific for the regimen which warms the organs of the sperm, carries good blood to them, and strengthens them, and fortifies erection.[194]

One should also attempt to constantly drink iron water, as is done by someone suffering from constipation, which is called *sachag.*[195] One should cool it and drink it when necessary. If it is possible that the broth of every food one consumes be iron water, then this is more powerful in fortifying erection and strengthening all the internal organs (than any other broth).

And know that physicians only consider ox-tongue[196]

juice as a drink which rejoices. The ancients have already tested this, that is, one soaks some ox tongue in wine and allows it to remain therein until its strength is extracted. They[197] discovered that (this drink) greatly increases one's rejoicing and adds to sexual intercourse. And if one takes some of the well-known iron water and boils therein four drachms of ox tongue, and half an ounce of lemon peel,[198] and half a drachm of crushed carnation,[199] and pours two liters of wine into this water, or a liter of bee's honey for one who is not permitted wine,[200] and (if one) drinks a little[201] at a time of this (concoction), it will be of great benefit.

This amount (of information regarding aphrodisiac regimens) will suffice for that which was indicated to the Servant.[202] And let the Master[203] choose from this (treatise) that (regimen) which is easy (for him) to carry out, and do it time after time.[204] And may the Lord lengthen his days with pleasures, and may those delights be attached to eternal delights for the sake of His kindness and His goodness. (Amen.)[205] And blessed be the Lord the Savior.

Completed is the treatise (and concluded is the book, Praise to the Lord and glory to the Lord of Israel).[206]

Translation of Rabbi Zerachiah, the son of Rabbi Yitzhak, the son of Shealtiel Chen, from the city of Barcelona.[207]

Notes

1. The Codex Granada, which is written by an Islamic copyist begins as follows: "In the name of G'd the merciful, the Lord bless our Master Muhammed and his worshipers . . ."
2. lit: coitus.
3. Maimonides.
4. See Maimonides, *Eight Chapters* (edited by J. I. Gorfinkle; New York, Columbia Univ. Press, 1912, pp. 85–86), where he

states ". . . a man whose natural constitution inclines towards dryness . . . finds it much easier to learn, remember and understand things . . . In exactly the same way, he whose blood is somewhat warmer . . ." In addition, the Talmud in Tractate *Yoma* 18a discusses foods and beverages which should not be given to the High Priest immediately before the Day of Atonement lest he become sexually excited and polluted by elimination of semen, which would render him unfit for the service on the Day of Atonement on the morrow. Also in Tractate *Sanhedrin* 39b we find: "Ahab was frigid by nature, so Jezebel painted pictures of two harlots on his chariot, that he might look upon them and become heated." See also First Kings 1, 2: "Let there be sought for my Lord the King a young virgin; and let her stand before the King and be a companion unto him; and let her lie in thy bosom, that my Lord the King may get heat." See also Genesis 30, 39: "And the sheep became excited before the rods . . ."

5. lit: gather or collect.
6. lit: easily found.
7. lit: precede according to his honor.
8. The Talmud already described the great value of certain foods and aphrodisiacs many centuries before Maimonides; see Tractate *Yoma* 18a (footnote #4 above). Also Tractate *Baba Kamma* 82a: "Our Rabbis taught: Five things were said of garlic: It satiates, it keeps the body warm, it brightens the face, it increases semen, and it kills parasites in the bowels. Some say that it fosters love and removes jealousy." Maimonides himself, in his *Guide for the Perplexed* (Section 3, Chapters 33 and 49), discusses the relationship of foods to sexual intercourse.
9. The Paris manuscript omits the phrase "in reality."
10. Semen being a superfluity of food is a concept dating back to Hippocrates. Avicenna also describes this thesis of *sperma est superfluitas digestionis quartae, quae fit, cum dispartitur cibus in membris, resudando a venis, tertia digestione jam expleta et est de summa humiditas proximal coagulationi* . . . According to Galen, there are three stages of digestion: the first occurs in the stomach, the second takes place in the liver where nutriments are converted into blood, and the third is in the target organs to which blood and nutriments are supplied.

11. The last phrase of this chapter in the Paris manuscript is unclear. Thus, the translation was made from the Arabic and Munich Hebrew manuscripts.
12. i.e., to increase sexual potency.
13. See the Talmud, Tractate *Sotah* 7a, where the suspected adulteress is confronted by the judges who state ". . . My daughter, wine does much, frivolity does much . . ." in an attempt to excuse her behavior. Also Tractate *Aboth* (Ethics of the Fathers) 3, 17, where Rabbi Akiba states: "Jesting and levity lead a man on to lewdness."
14. The order differs somewhat in the various manuscripts.
15. See the Talmud, Tractate *Kiddushin* 80b, where it is stated: ". . . in the time of grief, one's passions are subdued."
16. The Munich and Parma manuscripts substitute: "will dry the sperm."
17. Gorlin quotes Seidel (see Bibliography) who elucidates this by stating that there are men who copulate for a specific reason, without lust, pleasure or desire. As an example Seidel cites the Moslem custom of marrying an unloved woman solely to produce an heir. Other examples are marriages of state or convenience.
18. The Munich manuscript omits "the elimination," thus making the phrase unintelligible.
19. lit: Pharisees—i.e., Nazarites, ascetics and the like.
20. Hebrew: *Aziva*, lit: abstention or something best left alone. See the Talmud Tractate *Nedarim* 22a, where it states: "If her mother had not seen something shameful (i.e., licentiousness; lit: something best left alone) in her behavior . . ." A story is told of Rabbi Eleazar Ben Dordia who was addicted to immorality (Tractate *Abodah Zarah* 17a). Divine forgiveness came when Eleazar did penitence. A similar tale is related in Tractate *Menachoth* 44a.
21. coitus.
22. Kroner has "instinctive."

22a. Arabic Ms: *falu elikhtiza au fa'l ennamu.*

23. lit: living soul, i.e., *vis animalis*—See Maimonides, *Eight Chapters* (note 4 above), where, in the first chapter, he describes the soul and its powers, its activities and its parts (nutritive, perceptive, imaginative, appetitive and rational).
24. lit: happenings of the soul.
25. lit: a powerful movement.

26. see Tractate *Sotah* 42a, where it states: "Rabbi Eleazar also said: Any community in which is flattery is as repulsive as a menstruant woman . . ."
27. Avicenna (III, 20 F.556) mentions all except the last one of these types of women.
28. This last phrase is somewhat unclear in the various manuscripts. Kroner (1916) translates: "with a repulsive woman in whom menstruation has ceased because she imposes abstention," which amends his earlier (1906) version "with a woman who is abhorred because nature (i.e., menses) has ceased."
29. The Munich manuscript substitutes: "nature will gather laziness."
30. lit: praiseworthy.
31. The Munich manuscript substitutes: "cattle meat."
32. The Munich manuscript substitutes: "young doves."
33. lit.: rooster eggs (hormone therapy?).
34. lit: the brain of bones.
35. Here the word "eggs" is to be taken literally.
36. The Paris manuscript has the word *Parditz;* the Munich manuscript has the word *Koreh,* both meaning partridge. The Parma and Sacre Monte Arabic manuscripts omit this word entirely. In Maimonides' *Commentary on the Mishnah,* in Tractate *Hullin* 12,2, he states: "*Koreh* is a well-known bird whose name is *Parditz* (Partridge; *perdix* in Latin)."
37. The Arabic manuscript substitutes: "sparrow eggs."
38. The Munich manuscript has "breasts." Kroner translates "udders." The Parma manuscript omits the last three words of this sentence.
39. *Brassica napus L.*
40. *Lactuca Scariola L.* This must be an error in the Arabic and Paris Hebrew manuscripts, since in Chapter five of this work, Maimonides considers lettuce to be an anaphrodisiac. The Munich and Parma manuscripts omit it here.
41. *Allium cepa L.*
42. *Foeniculum vulgare L.*
43. *Mentha piperita Smith.*
44. *Atriplex hortensis L.*
45. *Vicia faba L.*
46. *Vigna Sinensis Endl.*, also known as *Dolichos Lablab (Lubia) L.*

47. *Sesamum orientale.*
48. *Asparagus officinalis L.*
49. Amygdalus.
50. *Corylus avellana L.*
51. *Pistacia vera L.*
52. *Pistacia terebinthus L.*
53. *Cocos nucifera L.*
54. The Parma and Munich manuscripts have *Hab Al Zalam.* The Arabic manuscript omits the words "meaning *Al Zalna.*"
55. *Cyperus esculentus L.*, or *Cyperus rotundus L.*
55a. This sentence is lacking in the Arabic manuscript.
56. The Arabic and Munich Hebrew manuscripts reverse the order and read "medicine or food."
57. The Munich manuscript substitutes an unintelligible phrase here.
58. lit: widens the soul. See Psalms 104,15: "And wine maketh glad the heart of man"; and Ecclesiastes 10,19: ". . . And wine maketh glad the life . . ."
59. Here Maimonides makes no apologies for recommending wine, which is forbidden by Moslem law, to a Sultan. Yet in three of his other works, Maimonides finds it necessary to justify and defend his prescription of wine. 1) Bar-Sela, A., H. E. Hoff and E. Faris. *Moses Maimonides' Two Treatises on the Regimen of Health* (Trans. Amer. Philos. Soc., July 1964) p. 40, where Maimonides states: "Let not our Master censure his minor Servant for what he has mentioned in this his treatise about the use of wine and song, both of which the (Moslem) Law abhors, because this servant has not commanded that this ought to be done, but mentioned what his Art determines . . . The physician, because he is a physician, must give information on the conduct of a beneficial regimen, be it unlawful or permissible, and the sick have the option to act or not to act . . ." 2) *Ibid.*, p. 19. "It is known among all physicians, that the best of all nutriments is that which was prohibited in Islam (i.e., wine). It combines the laudable qualities of all foods, because it nourishes with good, abundant, and delicate nourishment, it is quick to be digested, . . . It has other virtues besides these . . . But words about that which is illicit are futile . . ." 3) Muntner, S., *Treatise on Asthma; The Medical Writings of Moses Maimonides* (Philadelphia: J. B. Lippincott,

1963), pp. 31–32: "Having discussed the nature of the foods suitable for Your Highness, I will say a few words about beverages, although most of them I do not apply to Moslems for whom wine is forbidden . . . but it is the amount (of wine) which is to blame . . . a small quantity, some 3 or 4 glasses of wine taken at the time the food is digested . . . is quite useful in the diet of the healthy and an excellent cure for many disorders . . . It is no use, though, to enumerate the good points of a thing whose enjoyment is out of the question where Your Highness is concerned . . . Since it is forbidden to Moslems in either large or small amounts, physicians have taken pains to put at their disposal similar beverages. Here belongs the honeyed drink . . ."

Later in the *Treatise on Sexual Intercourse* (Chapter 10), Maimonides also offers a honey electuary as a substitute for wine to those for whom wine is forbidden.

60. The filling of the vessels in the penis.
61. lit: intention.
62. i.e. flatulence.
63. *Ruta graveolens L.*
64. *Cuminum cyminum L.*
65. *Nigella sativum L.*
66. *Carum carvi L.*
67. *Polygonum hydropiper L; piper montanum.*
68. *Sinapis* or *Brassica alba* and *nigra L.*
69. *Piper longus L.*
70. *Alpinia Galanga Sw.;* resembles ginger.
71. Kroner's German translation erroneously has "one ounce each."
72. *Cinnamomum aromaticum Ness.*
73. *Pimpinella anisum L.*
74. *Myristica fragrans Houtt.*
75. The original Arabic manuscript adds here: "according to the will of his Royal Majesty, the Lord G'd." The Munich and Paris #335 Hebrew manuscripts substitute an unintelligible phrase.
76. *Lens esculenta Moench.*
77. *Lathyrus sativus L.* Kroner translates "ceratoma" from the Hebrew, and "vetch" from the Arabic; Seidel translates "peas."

78. Kroner translates "fresh vegetables."
79. *Artemisia vulgaris L.* The Munich manuscript has the word *Ketof* here which is *atriplex hortensis L.*
80. Either *Euspongia officinalis* or *spinacia oleracea L.*
81. See note 40 above.
82. *Cucumis sativus L.* and *cucumis melo* L.
83. *Citrullus vulgaris L.*
84. *Brassica Rapa L.*, in the Arabic codex: *al kunb;* another version: *al luft.*
85. *Nymphaea Lotus L;* the water lily.
86. The Munich, Parma Hebrew and the Granada Arabic manuscripts have "combinations of foods" before "compounded medications."
87. The Munich and Granada manuscripts have "two year old."
88. *Atriplex hortensis L.*
89. *Daucus carota L.* Some manuscripts have "pastinaca."
90. In the previous chapter.
91. lit: their flavor should be felt or tasted.
92. Some manuscripts have rooster testicles.
93. Some manuscripts have young pigeons.
94. lit: measured or estimated or calculated.
95. Arabic word meaning "a food preparation."
96. Or sheep.
97. Or rooster testicles.
98. A solid measure. Only the Paris Hebrew Ms #335 reads one quarter drachma, a different measure.
99. *Dianthus cariofilum L.*
100. Alternate translation: ten eggs.
101. lit: strengthens the brain.
102. Kroner translates "sparrows."
103. *Daucus carota.*
104. Avicenna.
105. Kroner quotes the original Arabic text from Avicenna for this as well as the previous food concoction.
106. lit: cooked.
107. *Scincus officinalis*, a type of lizard. Kroner translates "crocodile."
108. *Oleum sesamum.* lit: sesame juice.
109. lit: eggs.
110. In the Arabic version (1916), Kroner translates "sparrow

brains." In the Hebrew version (1906), he omits it entirely, although both the Munich and Parma manuscripts contain the phrase "3 ounces of bird brains."

111. Some manuscripts have sheep.
112. lit: hearts of pine. Kroner translates "peeled pine."
113. lit: hearts of pistachio.
114. *Amygdalae dulces.* Kroner translates "peeled almonds."
115. gingelly in English; *jugeoline* in French; *zuzzolino* in Italian; and *aljonjoli* in Spanish.
116. *Eruca sativa Mill.*
117. i.e., it congeals to sweetness.
118. *Daucus carota.*
119. *Pastinaca Schekakul Russ.* or *pastinaca dissecta Vent.* The Parma manuscript and Kroner interpret *saqaqil* as *Eryngium campestre L.* (sea-holly root.)
120. Kroner translates "preparation."
121. lit: upper.
122. Carrot or *saqaqil.*
123. *lingua avis.* The fruit of the *Fraxinus excelsier L.* tree.
124. Root of the *Statice limonium L.*
125. Root of the *Centaurea Behen L.*
126. *Alpinia officinarum Hance* or *Alpinia Galanga Willd.*
127. *Piper longum.*
128. The sequence of these spices varies in the different manuscripts.
129. *Curcuma Zedoaria Rosc.*
130. *Commiphora.* Kroner translates "caryophyllum," since some manuscripts have the word *shekelmor* (caryophyllum) rather than the two words *mishkal mor* (a *mishkal* of myrrh).
131. A type of lizard or crocodile. See note 107 above.
132. The Biblical manna is referred to here. An excellent study of manna and what it represents was published by Alfred Kaiser in Switzerland in 1924 under the title *Der Heutige Stand des Mannafrage.* Kaiser traveled to the Sinai desert in the pursuit of his investigations and concludes that manna is derived from a tamarisk tree, specifically the *Tamarix Nilotica Ehromb, var. mannifera.* For a further discussion of the source of manna, see Max Meyerhof, *Sarh Asma Al Uqqar* (*L'Explication Des Noms De Drogues*), *Un Glossaire de Matière Médicale Composé par Maimonide* (Mem. Inst. d'Egypte, 1940), pp. 193–194.

133. Caryophyllum. Kroner has "ground carnation."
134. The Parma and Munich Hebrew manuscripts as well as the Granada Arabic manuscripts have "five drachms each."
135. *Asparagus officinalis L.*
136. *Pastinaca schekakul Russ.* The Parma manuscript substitutes *Eryngium campestre L.*
137. *Zingiber zerumbet Rose.*
138. See notes 124 and 125.
139. *Scilla maritima.*
140. Possibly referring to the stomach or intestines.
141. *Medicago sativa.* In Spanish *yerba de mula.*
142. *Urtica pilulifera L.* and *Urtica urens L.*, the stinging nettle. Galen in Chapter six of his book *Simple Remedies* had already mentioned the aphrodisiac efficacy of imbibing nettles in wine.
143. *Raphanus sativus.*
144. The Munich manuscript substitutes one drachm and the Granada Arabic manuscript has sixty drachms.
145. The Parma manuscript omits "four drachms of cinnamon" and the Munich manuscript substitutes "one takes four drachms thereof."
146. The sequence in the Arabic manuscript as well as some of the Hebrew manuscripts differs somewhat.
147. *Corylus avellana L.* Ponticon.
148. Crotolaria.
148a. The Arabic manuscript adds here: by the pharmacist.
149. *Xylo-balsamom, succedaneum.*
150. *Cyperus escullentus L.*
151. *Pistacia terebintus L.*
151a. The Hebrew manuscripts substitute one half portion.
152. A type of flat cake. Alternate translation ". . . kneaded with panise (or panic, a type of grain) . . ."
153. *Brassica Napus L. var. esculenta.'*
154. Kroner, translating from both the Arabic and Munich Hebrew manuscripts, has "carrots."
155. *Ficus carica.*
156. lit: cooked a good cooking.
157. Kroner again, from the Munich and in the Arabic manuscripts, adds ". . . in this filtrate one adds depitted raisins, cooks it well, strains it and upon this . . ."

158. lit: until there remains wine.
159. The Arabic manuscript reads: "Similarly Ali has mentioned . . ." probably referring to Abu Ali Ibn Sina (Avicenna).
160. The *membrum virile bovis.* The Munich manuscript has "dried ox penis."
161. The Arabic manuscript inserts here ". . . and dry it . . ."
162. The Granada Arabic and Munich Hebrew manuscripts substitute "The meaning of . . ."
163. Scincus, a type of lizard. *Istinak* in Arabic.
164. See note 140.
165. Stomach and intestines.
166. Alternate translation: And he will be greatly strengthened.
167. *Phoenix dactilifera. Alnacal* in Arabic.
168. In Chapter 20 of Maimonides' *Medical Aphorisms* (see Muntner, S. *Pirke Moshe Birefuah;* Jerusalem, Mossad Harev Kook, 1959, pp. 238–240), he gives a lengthy quotation from Ibn Zohr (Avenzoar). Excerpts are as follows: ". . . Fowl is beneficial for feebleness, hemiplegia, paresis, and the pain of edema. It also increases sexual potential . . . Testicles of all living creatures are warming and moistening (in their action) and aid the libido in a strongly perceptible manner . . . Pigeon eggs are good aphrodisiacs. Similarly, all eggs help the libido, especially if they are cooked with onion or turnip . . . Palm hearts, namely, that which is called *Al Harioth* (in Arabic, or *karyotos* in Greek) gives rise to much bad semen and also helps sexual intercourse . . ."
169. *orchis morio*—Kroner has "Satyrion."
170. *Lingua bovis, Anchusa officinalis L; Borago officinalis L.*
171. Ferula; *Donema ammoniacum Don.*
172. Scincus.
173. apple wine or cider.
174. Both Paris Hebrew manuscripts (#1173 and #335), the Munich Hebrew manuscript and the Granada Arabic manuscript all have "They." The Parma manuscript has "He" which seems more logical. The "He" may refer to Avenzoar or to Maimonides himself.
175. Kroner translates: who have no sperm. Gorlin translates: whose sperm flow has been decreased by ejaculation. Another possible translation: who desire to prolong erection by not ejaculating.

176. The Munich and Granada manuscripts have "glans penis."
177. The Munich manuscript substitutes: another medication is . . .
178. feverfew?; *Anacyclus pyrethrum DC; Peucedanum venetum.* The Talmud (Tractate *Gittin* 69a) already makes mention of this herb when it states: "Rabbi Johanan said that for swollen glands, pellitory (feverfew) leaves are as good as *mamru* . . ."
179. *Euphorbia resinifera Berg.*
180. Paris Manuscript # 1120 has the earthen musk or *Origanum dictammes L.* In general, musk refers to *Commiphora myrrha Engl.*
181. *Jasminum sambax Vahl.*
182. The Munich Hebrew manuscript reads: "the pubic symphysis and below, between the thighs and the penis and the testicles." The Granada Arabic manuscript reads: "the pubic hair, the flanks, the testicles and the penis." Kroner incorrectly translates penis as urethra.
183. The Munich and Granada manuscripts have the word "medicaments" before the word "foods."
184. The Munich and Granada manuscripts have "musk."
185. *Spondias magnifera Willd; Liquidamber orientalis.*
186. *Myristica muscata Thung.* Kroner omits "Galia" as does the Munich manuscript.
187. The Munich and Granada manuscripts insert here: "they (the feet) become dry."
188. The Munich, Parma and Granada manuscripts have "coccyx," or last bone in the vertebral column.
189. "with much butter" is omitted in the Munich and Granada manuscripts.
190. lit: end.
191. i.e., a warming medication.
192. The coccygeal area.
193. Alternately: musk.
194. The Parma, Munich and Granada manuscripts all have slightly different versions from the one given in this book (Paris #1173).
195. *Sachag* is colitis. Colitis is usually associated with diarrhea, occasionally with constipation. Thus, some manuscripts omit the word "constipation."

196. *Lingua bovis.*
197. The ancient physicians.
198. *Citrus medica.*
199. *Dianthus caryophyllus.*
200. Moslem. See note 59 above.
201. The Munich manuscript substitutes "first" for "little."
202. Maimonides.
203. The Sultan.
204. Alternate meaning: sometimes the one, other times, another.
205. Each manuscript ends slightly differently. The version given here is from the Parma and Paris (#1173) manuscripts.
206. The Arabic manuscript ends with the following phrase: "Most praised be the Lord as He should be, and may G'd bless our Master Muhammed, his followers and his friends and give them happiness."
207. The Parma manuscript omits this last sentence. The Paris manuscript #1173 ends with a song of praise of Maimonides written by Rabbi Yudah Halevi; the Paris manuscript #1120 ends with a recipe by Maimonides' son Abraham.

Excerpts on Sex from Maimonides' Other Writings

Maimonides' Treatise on Hemorrhoids

Maimonides' *Treatise on Hemorrhoids* was written for a nobleman—as Maimonides says in the Introduction—probably a member of the Sultan's family. There are seven chapters dealing with normal digestion, foods harmful to patients with hemorrhoids, beneficial foods, and general and local therapeutic measures, such as sitz baths, oils and fumigations. Maimonides disapproves of bloodletting or surgery for hemorrhoids except in very severe cases. Maimonides' whole approach to the problem seems to bespeak a modern medical trend. The *Treatise on Hemorrhoids* was first published by Kroner in 1911 in Arabic, Hebrew and German (1). A good general description of the work in English appeared in 1927 by Bragman (2). The definitive Hebrew edition is that of Muntner dated 1965 (3) and an English translation of the entire work was recently published by Rosner and Muntner (4).

In the introduction to this work, Maimonides describes the reason for writing it:

> There was a youth (descended) from knowledgeable, intelligent and comprehending forebears, from a promi-

nent and renowned family, distinguished and charitable and of great means, in whom the affliction of hemorrhoids occurred at the mouth of the rectum, that interested me in his problem and placed the task (of healing them) upon me. These irritated him on some occasions and he treated them in the customary therapeutic manner until the pain subsided and the prolapsed rectum (literally: excesses that protruded) became reduced and returned to the interior of the body so that his (bodily) functions returned to normal. Because this (illness) recurred many times, he considered having them extirpated in order to uproot this malady from its source so that it not return again. I informed him of the danger inherent in this, in that it is not clear if these hemorrhoids (literally: additions) are of the variety which should be excised or not, since there are people in whom they have once been (surgically) extirpated and in whom other hemorrhoids develop. This is because the causes which give rise to the original ones remained and therefore new ones develop.

Here Maimonides provides an insight into the etiology of disease in general in that he regards operative excision of hemorrhoids with skepticism, because surgery does not remove the underlying causes which produced the hemorrhoids in the first place.

1. Kroner, H., "Die Hämorrhoiden in der Medizin des XII und XIII Jahrhunderts," *Janus* 16, 1911, pp. 441–456, 644–718.
2. Bragman, L.J., "Maimonides' Treatise on Hemorrhoids," *New York State Med. J.*, 27, 1927, pp. 598–601.
3. Muntner, S., *Moshe ben Maimon. On Hemorrhoids* (Birefuoth Hatechorim). Jerusalem: Mossad Harav Kook, 1965. 32 pp. (Hebr.)
4. Rosner, F., and S. Muntner, *Treatise on Hemorrhoids and Maimonides' Answers to Queries. The Medical Writings of*

Fred Rosner

Moses Maimonides. Philadelphia: Lippincott, 1969. XV and 79 pp.

Extract from Maimonides' *Treatise on Hemorrhoids*

(See F. Rosner, and S. Muntner, *Treatise on Hemorrhoids and Responsa, The Medical Writings of Moses Maimonides.* Philadelphia: J.B. Lippincott Co., 1969. XV and 79 pp.)

Chapter 1 (p.5)

. . . any movement immediately after a meal interferes with digestion; that is, any movement, such as the movement of physical exercise or the activity of coitus or bathing or mental excitement . . .

Maimonides' Treatise on the Regimen of Health

Maimonides wrote his *Regimen of Health (Regimen Sanitatis)* in 1198, during the first year of the reign of Sultan Al Malik Al Afdal, eldest son of Saladin the Great. The Sultan was a frivolous and pleasure-seeking man of thirty, subject to fits of melancholy or depression due to his excessive indulgences in wine and women, as well as his warlike adventures against his own relatives and in the Crusades. He complained to his physician of constipation, dejection, bad thoughts and indigestion. Maimonides answered his royal patient in four chapters. The first chapter is a brief abstract on diet taken mostly from Hippocrates and Galen. The second chapter deals with advice on hygiene, diet and drugs in the absence of a physician. The third extremely important chapter contains Maimonides' concept of "a healthy mind in a healthy body," perhaps the first description of psychosomatic medicine. He indicates that the physical well-being of a person is dependent on his mental well-being and vice versa. The final chapter summarizes his prescriptions relating to climate, domicile, occupation, bathing, sex, wine drinking, diet and respiratory infections.

The whole treatise on the *Regimen of Health* is short and concise but to the point. This is the reason for its great success and popularity throughout the years. It is extant in numerous manuscripts. A Hebrew translation from the original Arabic was made by Moses ben Samuel Ibn Tibbon in 1244 and this version was reprinted several times in the nineteenth century (Prague 1838, Jerusalem 1885, Warsaw 1886). Two Latin translations were made in the thirteenth century. Several fifteenth-century incunabulae and sixteenth-century editions of these Latin versions exist. A French translation by Carcousse appeared in 1887 in Algiers (1). The Arabic text with German and Hebrew translations was published by Kroner in 1925 (2), although he had already published the all-important Chapter 3 dealing with psychosomatic medicine eleven years earlier, in 1914 (3). An English translation of Chapter 3 by Bragman appeared in 1932 (4). The definitive Hebrew edition is that of Muntner dated 1957 (5). Two English translations of the entire work were published: in 1958 by Gordon (6) and 1964 by Bar Sela, Hoff and Faris (7). Another German translation by Muntner appeared in 1966 (8). These numerous editions in many languages attest to the importance and popularity of Maimonides' *Regimen of Health.*

1. Carcousse, M., *Hygiene isráelite, principes de santé physique et morale de l'arabe par Arab Mouchi ben Mimoun.* Algiers, 1887. 51 pp.
2. Kroner, H., *Fi tadbit as sihhat. Gesundheitsanleitung des Maimonides für den Sultan al-Malik, al-Afdhal, Janus,* 27, 1923, pp. 101–116, 286–330; 28, 1924, pp. 61–74, 143–152, 199–217, 408–419, 455–472; 29, 1925, pp. 235–258.
3. Kroner, H., *Die Seelenhygiene des Maimonides. Auszug aus dem 3. Kapital des diatetischen Sendschreibens des Maimonides an den Sultan al Malik Alafdahl (ca. 1198).* Frankfurt A.M.: J. Kauffmann, 1914. 18 pp. (Ger.), 8, pp. (Hebr. and Arab).

4. Bragman, L.J., "Maimonides on Physical Hygiene," *Ann. Med. Hist.*, 7, 1925, pp. 140–143.
5. Muntner, S., Moshe ben Maimon. *Hanhagath habriuth, Regimen sanitatis.* (Letters on the hygiene of the body and of the soul). Jerusalem: Mossad Harav Kook, 1956. XVIII and 254 pp. (Hebr).
6. Gordon, H.L., *Moses ben Maimon, The Preservation of Youth. Essays on Health (Fi Tadbir as-Sihha).* New York: Philos. Lib., 1958. 92 pp.
7. Bar Sela, A., H.E. Hoff, and E. Faris, *Moses Maimonides' Two Treatises on the Regimen of Health.* Philadelphia: Am. Philos. Soc. (Trans. n.s., Vol. 54, Pt. 4), 1964. 50 pp.
8. Muntner, S., *Regimen Sanitatis oder Dietetik für die Seele und den Körper mit Anhang der medizinischen Responsen und Ethik des Maimonides.* Basel: S. Karger, 1966. 208 pp.

Excerpts from Maimonides' *The Regimen of Health*

(See A. Bar Sela, H.E. Hoff, and E. Faris, *Moses Maimonides' Two Treatises on the Regimen of Health.* Philadelphia: Amer. Philos. Soc. Trans. n.s., New Series, Vol. 54 Part 4, 1964. 50 pp.)

Chapter 1 (p.18)

. . . any movement after the meal is most harmful; by that I mean no strenuous movement, no coitus, and no bath . . .

It is not proper to take food, or enter a bath, or copulate, or sleep, or exercise, until one takes account of himself and tries to expel the superfluities . . .

Chapter 4 (p.29)

The behavior of all men regarding coitus is known. And that is, that there is not one who uses it for the sake of the regimen of health, or for the sake of procreation, but merely for pleasure; thus they lust until fatigued, at all times, and at every opportunity. It is already manifest among those who know that coitus is detrimental to all men except those few whose temperament is such that a little of it does no harm. But men differ only in the degree of harm; among them are those whom it harms greatly, and among them are those whom it harms but little. Its harm to the young that are of moist temperament is little. Its harm to the old, the convalescent, and those of dry temperament is very great. Among the convalescents we have already seen some who copulated and died that very day, or suffered syncope and recurrence of fever, and died after a few days. On the whole, it is a pernicious matter for the sick and the convalescent, and very detrimental to the old and to all of dry temperament. It is improper for anyone to copulate before the food in the stomach is digested, or when hungry, or when thirsty, or in a state of inebriety, or after leaving the bath, or following exercise or before it, or for a day before bloodletting and for a day thereafter. Whoever desires the continuance of health should drive his thoughts from coitus all he can.

Maimonides' Commentary on the Aphorisms of Hippocrates

One of Maimonides' medical writings is the *Commentary on the Aphorisms of Hippocrates.* The famous aphorisms of Hippocrates were translated from the Greek into Arabic by Hunain Ibn Yitzchak in the ninth century. Maimonides wrote his commentary on this translation. Two incomplete Arabic manuscripts exist. A good medieval translation into Hebrew was made by Moses ben Samuel Ibn Tibbon. In this work, Maimonides strongly criticizes both Hippocrates and Galen where either of these Greeks differ from his own views. For example, in Chapter 5, Hippocrates is quoted as having said "a boy is born from the right ovary, a girl from the left," to which Maimonides remarks, "A man should be either prophet or genius to know this." The introduction to this work was edited in the original Arabic with two Hebrew and one German translations by Steinschneider in 1894 (1). The entire work was published by Hasida in 1935 (2) and again in a definitive edition by Muntner in 1961 (3). Recently, Bar Sela and Hoff have published Maimonides' interpretation of the first aphorism of Hippocrates (4). This is the famous aphorism which has been called the motto or credo of the art of medicine: "Life is short, and the art long, the occasion fleeting, experience fallacious and judgment difficult. The physician must not only be prepared to do what is right himself, but must also make the patient, the attendant and the externals cooperate."

1. Steinschneider, M., "Die Vorrede des Maimonides zu seinem Commentar über die Aphorismen des Hippokrates." *Ztschr. d. deutsch. Morgenland. Gesellsch.*, 48, 1894, pp. 213–234.
2. Hasida (Bocian), M.Z., *Perush Lepirke Abukrat shel Ha-Rambam.* Hassegullah (Jerusalem) 1934–5, Nos. 1–30 (Stencil; Hebr.)
3. Muntner, S., *Mosheh ben Maimon. Commentary on the Aphorisms of Hippocrates. Perush lepirkei Abukrat.* Jerusalem: Mossad Harav Kook, 1961. XIV and 166 pp. (Hebr.)
4. Bar Sela, A., and H.E. Hoff, "Maimonides' Interpretation of the First Aphorism of Hippocrates," *Bull. Hist. Med.*, 37; 1968, pp. 347–354.

Extracts from Maimonides'
Commentary on the Aphorisms of Hippocrates

(See S. Muntner, *Mosheh ben Maimon. Perush Lepirkei Abukrat.* Jerusalem: Mossad Harav Kook, 1961. XIV and 166 pp.)

Chapter 6:19 (p. 125)

Hippocrates: If a bone or cartilage or nerve or the soft portion of the jaw or the tip (i.e., foreskin) of the penis is severed, it will not grow back nor reunite.

Maimonides: "will not grow back" means that it will not be renewed if the wound is deep. If it was split, it will not reunite, for these are "dry" organs . . .

Chapter 6:30 (p. 129)

Hippocrates: A young boy does not suffer from arthritis before he has had sexual intercourse with a woman.

Maimonides: Galen has stated that sexual intercourse is in great part related to the development of arthritis but he does not clarify the cause for this. It is my opinion that the reason is that the feet have little flesh (i.e., musculature) but many nerves and veins, and they are exposed to the air (during intercourse). When the nerves in general are damaged during sexual intercourse because of the emptying of his strength and their becoming cold, then the damage to the nerves of the feet is even greater. We always observe that when the feet become cold, erection of the penis is diminished. This is the proof that the nerves are in some manner related to the development of arthritis in the feet.

Maimonides' Treatise on Asthma

Very interesting is the book of Moses Maimonides entitled *Treatise on Asthma.* The patient for whom this book was written suffered from violent headaches which prevented him from wearing a turban. The patient's symptoms began with a common cold, especially in the rainy season, forcing him to gasp for air until phlegm was expelled. The patient asked whether a change of climate might be beneficial. Maimonides, in thirteen chapters, explains the rules of diet and climate in general and those rules specifically suited to asthmatics. He outlines the recipes of food and drugs and describes the various climates of the Middle East. He states that the dry Egyptian climate is efficacious for sufferers from this disease and warns against the use of very powerful remedies.

Several Arabic, Hebrew and Latin manuscripts of this work exist (1). The first critical edition appeared in Hebrew in 1940, edited by Muntner (2). Additional manuscripts became available after World War II, and a corrected, improved and revised second Hebrew edition appeared in 1963 (3). Only three hundred copies of this edition were printed and thus a third edition was published by Muntner in 1965 (4). An English version of Maimonides' book on asthma was published in 1963 (5) and a French translation in 1965 (6).

The last chapter of this work deals with concise admonitions and aphorisms which Maimonides considered "useful to any man desirous of preserving his health and administering to the sick." The chapter begins as follows: "The first thing to consider . . . is the provision of fresh air, clean water and a healthy diet." Fresh air is described in some detail: ". . . City air is stagnant, turbid and thick, the natural result of its big buildings, narrow streets, the refuse of its inhabitants . . . one should at least choose for a residence a wide-open site . . . living quarters are best located on an upper floor . . . and ample sunshine . . . Toilets should be located as far as possible from living rooms. The air should be kept dry at all times by sweet scents, fumigation and drying agents. The concern for clean air is the foremost rule in preserving the health of one's body and soul." Let our air pollution control programers take cognizance of Maimonides' prophetic statements nearly eight hundred years ago.

1. Rosner, F., "Maimonides' Treatise on Asthma," *Med. Times,* 94, 1926, pp. 1227–1230.
2. Muntner, S., *Moshe ben Maimon* (Maimonides) *Sefer hakatzereth* (The Book on Asthma). Jerusalem: Rubin Mass, 1940. XV and 168 pp. (Hebr.).
3. Muntner, S., *Rabbi Moses ben Maimon. Sefer hakatzereth or Sefer hamisadim* (The Book on Asthma). Jerusalem: Geniza, 1963. 56 pp. (Hebr.).
4. Muntner, S., *Moshe ben Maimon on Asthma (Sefer Hakatzereth).* Jerusalem: Mossad Harav Kook, 1965, pp. 67–119 (Hebr.)
5. Muntner, S., *Treatise on Asthma. The Medical Writings of Moses Maimonides.* Philadelphia: Lippincott, 1963, XXIV and 115 pp.
6. Muntner, S., and I. Simon, "Le Traité de L'asthme de Maimo-

nide (1135–1304) traduit pour la première fois en français d'après le texte hébreu," *Rev. d'hist. med. héb.*, 16, 1963, pp. 171–186; 17, 1964, pp. 5–13, 83–97, 127–139, 187–196; 18, 1965, pp. 5–15.

Extracts from Maimonides' *Treatise on Asthma*

(See S. Muntner, *Treatise on Asthma, The Medical Writings of Moses Maimonides.* Philadelphia. J. B. Lippincott Co., 1963. XXIV and 115 pp.)

Chapter 1:3 (p.7)

No physician of antiquity included in his general health regime the regulation of coitus. However, Hippocrates mentioned it in his diet for sick people when it becomes important, in the case of some bad constitutions, to conserve the semen outflow. But in most cases people indulge in it without any cause, other than from lust. To my mind, regulation of coitus should be included (in any regimen of health).

Chapter 5:6 (p. 26)

The symptoms appearing upon insufficient and bad digestion are as follows: a sense of repletion, heartburn, loose stool or frequent diarrhea, impotence . . .

Chapter 10:9 (p. 52)

Regarding coitus it is well known, even to the general public, that it is harmful to most people and, when indulged in to excess, is injurious to all of them. Discharge of semen as such is not counted among the salutary precepts of hygiene, except with a limited number of people with a wrong juice combination who change as time goes on. Along with the semen vital juices cannot help escaping from the body, so that its chief organs dry up and cool gradually. Only young men bear well this unavoidable nuisance, although even among them many pay for it with sickness. In any case, to old people coitus is at all times harmful, since they are dependent on anything that increases their natural warmth and keeps their organs properly humid, while coitus tends to extinguish and sap their strength little by little, as we pointed out above. A man of advanced age should therefore abstain from its exercise, the more strictly the better. All this is part of a healthy hygiene. Besides, this is also tied up with questions of keeping the body free of infections, purification of the spirit and of acquiring virtues through continence, modesty, and piety. If we say of coitus that it has an injurious effect on all organs, it is especially true with regard to the brain because the main discharge has to do with this part of the body. All this has been discussed by Hippocrates. This is why it is so important for anyone suffering from repeated headache to keep away from coitus. A man given to excessive exercise of coitus is found on inspection to suffer from (premature) lapses of memory and mental debility, with faulty digestion combined with green sickness, defective vision and bad appearance. There is a good reason for it, and, since human behavior varies greatly as well as human temperaments, there are admittedly some people, indifferent or subject to bad humor or defective digestion, who actually happen to regain by it their vitality, cheerfulness, and good appetite, while others experience just the opposite. People's peculiarities vary much in this respect. Galen described one of the bad aspects of this problem, saying: There is a physical phenomenon which should be regarded as very unfortunate, namely, that some people seem to produce a lot of warm semen which keeps them permanently excited and eager to discharge it. When they do discharge it, their stomach as well as their entire organism weaken, they dry up and grow lean, their looks deteriorate and their eyes sink deep in their sockets. Such people, even when they limit or suspend their coitus of their own accord because of the discomfort that comes over them, often suffer from a sense of heaviness in their head and pain in their stomach, which means that even continence brings them no relief. This results from the fact that they are harassed with nightly pollutions. Thus pollution causes them no less harm than coitus itself.

Chapter 10:10 (p.53)

Says the Author: My reason for mentioning the above was to draw attention to the various reactions of people in this respect. This book does not intend to offer medical details of all the cases involved and their treatment.

In short, Your Highness may carry on in this regard more or less as you are used to, but would do well to diminish your coitus little by little, as I said before, which is fitting in this disease and, depending on one's age, salutary for all people. Note: Coitus is bad for all people if it takes place soon after a bath or following physical exercise, at daybreak or within two days of the drinking of asparagus (a diaphoretic), to prevent two kinds of discharge (sweat, semen) from coinciding and enervating the organism all at once. Further, it is not advisable to have coitus when hungry, neither when the stomach is replete with food, but at the time the food has left the upper stomach and before hunger has set in again. The evil attending coitus on an empty stomach is much greater than that occurring in a state of repletion. The exercise of coitus while seriously ill is outright dangerous, even deadly. This I happened to observe myself, and also learned from reliable information that a man once had coitus while in acute fever, and his strength ebbed on that very day. He finally suffered a heart attack, and died on the following night.

Maimonides' Medical Answers (Responsa)

The ninth medical writing of Maimonides is the *Discourse on the Explanation of Fits (Responsa).* This work has been called Maimonides' swan song, as it probably is the last of his medical works, having been written in the year 1200, four years before his death. It was also written for the Sultan Al Malik Al Afdal and is sometimes considered to represent Chapter 5 of the *Regimen of Health.* The Sultan persisted in his overindulgences and wrote to Maimonides, who was himself ill, asking advice about his health. Maimonides confirms most of the prescriptions of the Sultan's other physicians regarding wine, laxatives, bathing, exercise and the like, and near the end, gives a very detailed hour-by-hour regimen for the daily life of the Sultan. The original Arabic was edited and published with Hebrew and German translations by Kroner in 1928 (1). English editions by Bar Sela, Hoff and Faris appeared in 1964 (2) and Rosner and Muntner in 1969 (3). Another German version by Muntner in 1966 (4) and another Hebrew edition by Muntner in 1969 (5) are available.

1. Kroner, H., "Der medizinische Schwanengesang des Maimonides," *Janus,* 32, 1928, pp. 12–116.

2. Bar Sela, A., H.E. Hoff, and E. Faris, *Moses Maimonides' Two Treatises on the Regimen of Health.* Philadelphia: Amer. Philos. Soc. (Trans. new series Vol. 54 Part 4), 1964. 50 pp.
3. Rosner, F., and S. Muntner, *Treatise on Hemorrhoids and Maimonides' Answers to Queries. The Medical Writings of Moses Maimonides.* Philadelphia: Lippincott, 1969. XV and 79 pp.
4. Muntner, S., *Regimen Sanitatis oder Dietetik für die Seele und den Körper mit Anhang der medizinischen Responsen and Ethik des Maimonides.* Basel: S. Karger, 1966. 208 pp.
5. Muntner, S., *Moshe ben Maimon. Biyur Shaymoth Harefuoth* (Lexicography of Drugs and Medical Responses). Jerusalem: Mossad Harav Kook, 1969. 164 pp.

Extracts from Maimonides' *Medical Answers (Responsa)*

(See F. Rosner and S. Muntner. *Treatise on Hemorrhoids and Responsa. The Medical Writings of Moses Maimonides.* Philadelphia: J.B. Lippincott Co., 1969. XV and 79 pp.)

Section #18 (p.54)

When our Master mentioned a reduction in coitus, notwithstanding the regular habit, this is a praiseworthy decision. How great is the benefit of such a reduction (to your Highness). Bathing, on the other hand, should under no circumstances be stopped . . .

Section #21:7 (p.69)

Regarding the time his (Highness) should have coitus, there are two times: one is following the digestion of the food after he has enjoyed a small quantity of wine before consuming the evening meal; the other, at the end of the night. The main point of this advice lies therein, that this act (coitus) should not occur while (one is) hungry, nor on an empty stomach, nor on a stomach replete with food . . .

Section #21:9 (p.70)

In the winter, he should diminish his coitus (compared to his usual habit) . . .

Maimonides' Code (Mishneh Torah)

The *Mishneh Torah* (Code of Maimonides) is undoubtedly Maimonides' magnum opus. In fourteen books, he compiled and organized in a lucid and systematic manner all of Biblical and Talmudic law. This work was written in clear Mishnaic Hebrew and is the only work of all of Maimonides' extensive writings not originally composed in Arabic. Philip Birnbaum, compiler of a recent abridged version of Maimonides' *Mishneh Torah,* states that it is "a repository of all Jewish teachings from the time of Moses, the lawgiver, to the time of Moses, the author of the *Mishneh Torah.* No detail escaped him in the vast Talmudic and post-Talmudic literatures. Unlike his predecessors and successors, Maimonides assembled all the ethical and civil regulations which the sages had deduced from the Bible. He took no account of whether the entire material which he incorporated into the *Mishneh Torah* was relevant to the conditions of his age. Thus he dealt with all the laws of Judaism, making no distinction between those regarding the Temple, the sacrifices, the Jewish kings, the Sanhedrin, and those which, for example, bear on the observance of the Sabbath or the practice of charity and prayer. Truly, the *Mishneh Torah* is the epitome of Judaism in all its varied aspects."

In the first book of Maimonides' *Mishneh Torah*, several chapters of the Laws of Temperaments *(Hilchoth De'oth)* deal nearly exclusively with principles of hygiene. Those passages describing sexual activities are excerpted below.

Excerpts from the Code of Maimonides

Laws of Temperaments

(See Maimonides' *Mishneh Torah, Hilchoth De'oth;* many editions are available.)

Chapter 3:2

. . . when a man eats and drinks and cohabits, he should not intend to do these things solely to obtain gratification therefrom to the point that he finds that he only eats and drinks that which is sweet to the palate, and cohabits for the pleasure thereof.. . . when he cohabits, he should not cohabit except to maintain the health of his body and to preserve his race (literally: his seed) . . .

Chapter 4:16

The manner of (correct) bathing is for a person to enter the bathhouse (and bathe) every seven days. One should not enter (the bath) immediately after eating, nor when one is hungry, but when the food begins to be digested. He should wash his entire body with hot water that will not scald the body, and the head alone (may be washed) with water hot enough to scald the body. Then he should wash his body with lukewarm water, and then with tepid water (and so on), until he washes with cold water. Over his head he should not pour either lukewarm or cold water. In the rainy (winter) season, one should not bathe in cold water. One should not bathe until one perspires and one's entire body becomes supple (from steam), nor should one remain too long in the bath; rather as soon as one perspires and the body becomes supple, one should rinse (the body) and leave (the bath).

One should examine oneself prior to entering the bath and after leaving it, lest excretion of wastes be necessary. A person should always similarly examine himself before meals and after meals, before sexual intercourse and after sexual intercourse, before and after he exercises and exerts himself, and before and after he goes to sleep. The total number of circumstances is thus ten.

Chapter 4:19

Effusion of semen represents the strength of the body and its life, and the light of the eyes. Whenever it (semen) is emitted to excess, the body becomes consumed, its strength terminates, and its life perishes. This is what Solomon in his wisdom stated: *Give not thy strength unto women* (Proverbs 31:3). He who immerses himself in sexual intercourse will be assailed by (premature) aging (based on the Talmud, Tractate *Shabbath* 152a). His strength will wane, his eyes will weaken, and a bad odor will emit from his mouth and his armpits. The hair of his head, his eyebrows, and eyelashes will fall out and the hair of his beard and armpits and the hair of his legs (will increase) excessively. His teeth will fall out and many maladies other than these will afflict him. The wise physicians have stated that one in a thousand dies from other illnesses and the (remaining 999 in the) thousand from excessive sexual intercourse. Therefore, a man must be cautious in this matter if he wishes to live wholesomely. He should not cohabit unless his body is healthy and very strong and he experiences many involuntary erections, and when he diverts (his thoughts) to another thing, the erection persists, and when he senses a heaviness from the loins and inferiorly as if the testicular cords are being tightened and his flesh is warm. Such (a person) requires coitus, and it is therapeutic for him to have sexual intercourse.

A person should not cohabit when he is satiated, nor when he is hungry, but after the food is digested in his intestines (based on Tractate *Nedarim* 20b). He should examine whether need for excretion (of urine or feces) exists, before coitus and after coitus. One should not have sexual intercourse standing or sitting, and not in a bathhouse, nor on the day when he takes a bath, nor on the day of phlebotomy, nor on the day when setting out on a journey or returning from a journey, nor on the previous or following (days of such occurrences) (based on Tractate *Gittin* 70a).

Chapter 5:4

Although a man's wife is always permitted to him, it is proper for a disciple of the wise to conduct himself with sanctity (based on Tractate *Shebuoth* 18b), and he should not be found with his wife like a rooster (based on Tractate *Berachot* 22a). Rather (he should cohabit) only on Friday nights (based on Tractate *Kethuboth* 62b), if he has the vigor. And when he converses with her, he should not converse at the beginning of the night when he is satiated and his stomach replete and not at the end of the night when he is hungry. Rather (he should cohabit) in the middle of the night when the food is digested in his intestines (based on Tractate *Nedarim* 20b). And he should not indulge excessively in frivolity, nor should he profane his mouth with vulgar talk even (if only) between him and her. For it is stated in Scripture: *And he related to man what his discourse is* (Amos 4:13), which our Sages interpreted (Tractate (*Chagigah* 5b) to mean: "Even for light discourse between a man and his wife will he in the future be called to judgment." And both of them (husband and wife) should not be intoxicated nor lazy nor melancholic (based on Tractate *Pesachim* 72b); nor either of them. And she should not be sleeping, and he should not coerce her if she is not willing (based on Tractate *Erubin* 100b). Rather (sexual intercourse should be carried out), with the consent of both, and while both are happy. He should converse and jest a little with her (based on Tractate *Berachoth* 72a), in order to put her at ease and he should then cohabit with modesty and not with impudence, and he should separate immediately.

Maimonides' Medical Aphorisms

Maimonides' medical work entitled the *Medical Aphorisms of Moses (Pirke Moshe Birefuah)* is the most voluminous of all. This book is comprised of 1500 aphorisms based mainly on Greek medical writers. There are twenty-five chapters, each dealing with a different area of medicine including anatomy, physiology, pathology, symptomatology and diagnosis, etiology of disease and therapeutics, fevers, bloodletting or phlebotomy, laxatives and emetics, surgery, gynecology, hygiene, exercise, bathing, diet, drugs and medical curiosities. A complete Arabic original manuscript exists in the Gotha library in East Germany. A Hebrew translation was made in the thirteenth century and published in Lemberg, Poland, in 1834 and again in Vilna in 1888 (1). The definitive Hebrew edition is that of Muntner dated 1959 (2). Maimonides' *Aphorisms* were also translated into Latin in the thirteenth century and appeared as an incunabulum in Bologna in 1489 and again in Venice in 1497 followed by numerous printed Latin editions. Only small fragments of this work have ever appeared in a Western language (3–6). A complete English version by Rosner and Muntner was recently published in two volumes (7–8).

A few excerpts from this most important work will give the reader the flavor of Maimonidean medical thinking. Maimonides speaks of cerebrovascular disease: "One can prognosticate regarding a stroke, called apoplexy. If the attack is severe, then he will certainly die but if it is minor, then cure is possible, though difficult . . . the worst situation that can occur following a stroke is the complete irreversible suppression of respiration . . ."

Maimonides seems to be describing diabetes when he states: "Individuals in whom sweet white [humor] occurs are very somnolent [hyperglycemia?]. To those who have an excess of sour white [humor], hunger occurs, then they become extremely thirsty. When this white liquid will be neutralized, then the thirst will disappear." Maimonides explains that diabetes mellitus was seldom seen in "cold" Europe, whereas it was frequently encountered in "warm" Africa. He also reports this disease to be associated with the imbibition of the sweet water of the Nile. (Maimonides lived in Fostat, or old Cairo.) There follows the English translation of this most important aphorism No. 69 from the eighth chapter: "Moses says: I too have not seen it in the West [Spain, where Maimonides was born and/or Morocco where he fled from the persecution of the Almohades] nor did any one of my teachers under whom I studied mention that they had seen it [diabetes]. However, here in Egypt, in the course of approximately ten years, I have seen more than twenty people who suffered from this illness. This brings one to the conclusion that this illness occurs mostly in warm countries. Perhaps the waters of the Nile, because of their sweetness, may play a role in this."

A very accurate description of obstructive emphysema is provided during a lengthy discussion of respiratory disease ". . . reason [for respiratory embarrassment] is narrowing of the organs of respiration, then the breast is seen to greatly expand. This expansion produces rapid and cut off [respirations] . . ."

Clubbing of the fingers associated with pulmonary disease is beautifully depicted: "With an illness affecting the lungs called *hasal*, namely, phthisis, there develops rounding of the nail as a rainbow." The signs and symptoms of pneumonia are remarkably accurately described: "The basic symptoms which occur in pneumonia and which are never lacking are as follows: acute fever, sticking [pleuritic] pain in the side, short rapid breaths, serrated pulse and cough mostly [associated] with sputum . . ." Hepatitis is just as beautifully described: "The signs of liver inflammation are eight in number as follows: high fever, thirst, complete anorexia, a tongue which is initially red and then turns black, biliary vomitus, initially yellow egg yolk in color which later turns dark green, pain on the right side which ascends up to the clavicle . . . Occasionally a mild cough may occur and a sensation of heaviness which is first felt on the right side and then spreads widely . . ."

Excerpted below are statements in the *Medical Aphorisms of Moses* dealing specifically with sex.

1. Magid, Z., *Medical Aphorisms of Maimonides (Pirke Moshe)*. Vilna: Lippman, 1888. 112 pp. (Hebr.). 1st ed., Lemberg, 1834.
2. Muntner, S., *Moshe ben Maimon.* (Medical) *Aphorisms of Moses in Twenty-five Treatises (Pirke Moshe Birefuah)*. Jerusalem: Mossad Harav Kook, 1959. XXXII and 470 pp. (Hebr.; Eng. summary).
3. Steinberg, W., and S. Muntner; "Maimonides' view on Gynecology and Obstetrics," *Am. J. Obst. Gynec.*, 91, 1965, pp. 443–448.
4. Rosner, F., and S. Muntner, "Moses Maimonides' Aphorisms Regarding Analysis of Urine," *Ann. Int. Med.*, 71: pp. 217–220, 1969.
5. Rosner, F., and S. Muntner, "The Surgical Aphorisms of Moses Maimonides," *Amer. J. Surg.*, 119, 1970, pp. 718–725.

6. Rosner, F., "Moses Maimonides and Diseases of the Chest," *Chest*, 60, 1971, pp. 68–72.
7. Rosner, F., and S. Muntner, *The Medical Aphorisms of Moses Maimonides.* Studies in Judaica. New York: Yeshiva Univ. Press, 1970, Vol. 1. 267 pp.
8. Rosner, F., and S. Muntner, *The Medical Aphorisms of Moses Maimonides.* Studies in Judaica. New York: Yeshiva Univ. Press, 1971, Vol. 2, 244 pp.

Excerpts from Maimonides' *Medical Aphorisms*

(See F. Rosner and S. Muntner. *The Medical Aphorisms of Moses Maimonides.* Studies in Judaica. New York: Yeshiva University Press. Vol. 1, 1970, 267 pp., and Vol. 2, 1971, 244pp.)

Chapter 1:72 (p.46)

The force in semen which can be found in material within blood is capable of making bones. It is material capable of making nerves and similar to other materials which make flat-appearing organs. This is called the *procreating force (vis generationis)*, since it gives birth to and generates material not previously present. It is also called the *developmental force* (*vis alterationis*). The force which gives shape and quality to that material until the bone has reached a certain size and a certain form as other flat-appearing organs (i.e., muscles, nerves, etc.) is called the *structure-forming force (virtus efformatrix).* It is the one which has a different origin, namely intellectual, in addition to its natural origin. The force which causes growth of that small bone and enables the small nerve to grow and mature is called the *growth force* (*auctrix*). The force which nourishes a limb until it grows and is able to eliminate superfluities is called the *nutritive force* (*nutrix*). It has four powers: attraction, retention, expulsion (of wastes) and alteration (of form). The power of alteration is also called the *digestive force*. It does not complete its function save through its powers of retention and assimilation.

Chapter 1:73 (p.46)

The procreating and structure-forming forces dominate as long as the fetus is still in the uterus, while the nutritive and growth forces are as their servants, ministering to them. Following birth, the structure-forming force ceases to exist, and the growth force dominates until the end of adolescence. At the same time, the nutritive force and the alteration power of the procreating force will help it, serve it and minister to it. At the end of adolescence, the growth and alteration forces cease and the nutritive one remains for the rest of one's life.

Chapter 3:2 (p.56)

The years between age 14 and 25 are the years of hair growth over the genitalia.

Chapter 3:12 (p.58)

The worst type of constitution is a dry temperament. This is understandable, since what occurs to old people through the course of many years is already present in them at the beginning of their lives. Sexual intercourse is one of the most damaging things in one whose constitution leans to the dry side.

Chapter 3:17 (p.59)

Semen and blood are of one constitution in the summer and a different constitution in the winter. Therefore, variations in fetuses occur in these (different) times, since the heat of summer dries and warms the semen whereas the cold of winter cools and moistens it.

Chapter 3:62 (p.70)

The penis, the genitalia and the cervix uteri possess an abundance of nerves necessary for sensation and feeling during coitus. The other organs of procreation include the corpus uteri, the two testicles of males and their adnexae, referring to the spermatic ducts. These only have small nerves similar to those which innervate other internal organs such as the liver, spleen and both kidneys.

Chapter 7:17 (p. 129)

He who has an excess of black bile in his body is very fond of sexual intercourse, because many strange flatulent gases accumulate in his body below the flanks (iliac or pubic areas).

Chapter 7:61 (p.140)

It is not surprising that he who indulges excessively in sexual intercourse becomes weak, because the entire body empties itself of pneuma and liquids. Added to this comes a pleasurable sensation which by itself can cause the cessation and weakening of life's strength. There are many in whom a sudden strong and strenuous pleasure leads to death.

Chapter 9:110 (p.196)

Concerning he who (suddenly) ceases from sexual intercourse who is usually accustomed to this activity, he (Galen) states: I have often seen their bodies become cold and their movements burdensome. In some of these (people), it goes so far that they become confused without any cause and this is mental confusion. This affliction which befalls them is similar to that which occurs to patients with black confusion (melancholia). All this occurs secondary to putrefaction of the retained semen, because it causes bad vapor to ascend.

Chapter 17:8

The indulgence in sexual intercourse is one of the requirements for the maintenance of health, providing that there should be adequate (intervals of) abstinence between periods of indulgence, so that no noticeable enfeeblement or weakness should ensue; rather one's body should feel lighter than before the act. During the time that one performs coitus, a person should not be filled with food, nor completely empty thereof, nor very cold nor very warm. The same applies to dryness and moisture. If one deviates from any of the aforementioned, then this deviation should be small. That is, the performance (of sexual intercourse) when (the stomach is) full, or at a time when the body is heated, or at a time that it is moist, is less damaging than its performance in situations where the reverse conditions prevail.

Chapter 17:9

Coitus always affects drying. However, he who has a vaporous superfluity in his body, whereby a bad, warm constitution prevails, will still obtain benefit therefrom. Only in this (type of) constitution is moderate indulgence in coitus salutary.

Chapter 17:10

For the preservation of health, a person should first perform physical exercise, and afterward strive for food and drink, and after that care for (the regulation of) sleep.

Chapter 17:11

One should ingest food after complete digestion of the previous meal, or after moderate physical exercise, or after the flatulence that arises therefrom has dissipated. One should pay heed not to take food prior to these, lest it be transported to the organs prior to its digestion. If one does take (food) while the intestines are filled with gases (flatulence), the head may become filled therewith, and in most instances a bloating is produced at the pylorus.

Chapter 17:12

After a person has exercised properly, and washed himself in the prescribed manner, and nourished himself with beneficial food, and then slept, he can, thereafter, indulge in sexual intercourse, if he so desires.

Chapter 17:13

No person is harmed from coitus except one whose body is warm and moist, or one whose nature is to produce warm semen. The greatest harm occurs in one whose constitution leans towards dryness and old age.

Chapter 17:14

There are some very bad activities among the characteristics of the body. That is, in many people, extremely warm, biting, sharp and irritating semen is produced, which stimulates them to eliminate it (the semen). When they eject it during coitus, then the pylorus of the stomach weakens, and their whole body becomes enfeebled. They dry up, become debilitated, their appearance changes, and their eyes become sunken in. If they indulge (in coitus) infrequently, their heads become heavy and their stomachs distressed, and they are harmed by abstaining from coitus, just as they sustain damage by indulging in coitus. The practice of such individuals, in my opinion, should be to abstain from anything that produces semen. They should consume foods and medications that suppress semen formation. They should do gymnastics involving the upper parts of their body, such as ball playing with either a small or large (ball), or lifting stones. They should rub the lower part of their spine with cooling oils, after bathing. If the desire is to eliminate semen, one should feed them favorable nourishment during the day, and also at the time of the evening meal. Just prior to going to sleep, they may indulge in coitus, and then go to sleep. Upon awakening, they should cool the body and rub it with towels, until the skin reddens. Then they should rub it to a moderate degree with oil, move a little, eat some toast dipped in diluted wine, and then they can go about their normal business.

Chapter 17:20

I advise all righteous people not to conduct themselves in the manner of many people who behave in animal-like custom, meaning the seeking of the most pleasurable (in life), and nothing else (hedonism). It seems more desirable that every person learn by experience which foods and which beverages and which activities harm him, and from which he should abstain. So too, he should test whether coitus is harmful and (if so), after how much time it is no longer harmful. He should then conduct himself accordingly and choose all that is of benefit to him according to his desires, and refrain from all that which might harm him. He who conducts himself in this manner will rarely need a physician and will always remain healthy.

Chapter 20:69

(The consumption of) fowl is beneficial for feebleness, hemiplegia, (facial) paresis, and the pain of edema. It also increases sexual potential. . . .

Chapter 20:71

Chicken testicles provide excellent nourishment. They are especially useful to nourish a weakened or convalescent individual. Testicles of all living creatures are warming and moistening (in their action), and aid the libido in a strongly perceptible manner.

Chapter 20:72

Pigeon eggs are good aphrodisiacs. Similarly, all eggs help the libido, especially if they are cooked with onion or turnip.

Chapter 20:86

Concerning the coconut, *Al Tamimi* contradicted what *Johanan Ibn Messue* declared, namely, that it warms and moistens and increases semen. *Al Tamimi* states that it warms and dries. It is bad because it produces black bile, and there is no good in it. He further stated that safflower has the special property of stimulating the desire for sexual intercourse. Similarly, anise cleanses white liquids from the uterus.

Chapter 22:50

If the virile member is rubbed with hedgehog fat, a strong and powerful erection is stimulated, and increased pleasure is derived from sexual intercourse. The hedgehog penis, if dried and pulverized and imbibed, also stimulates a strong erection. The same is accomplished with the penis of a ram, because of this specific property which lies therein.

Chapter 22:65

He further states that blossoms of the mountain ash tree stimulate women to desire coitus, to the point that what happens to cats occurs to them, in that they enjoy and rejoice even in just scenting this blossom.

Chapter 23:96

The cervix of the uterus and the neck of the womb are two synonyms for one and the same organ. The side of the cervix leading into the uterus is called the mouth of the womb (internal uterine orifice), and this is the one which is very tightly closed during pregnancy. The side leading to the vagina, into which the penis is inserted, is called the mouth of the neck of the uterus (external or cervical orifice).

Chapter 24:18

One should examine a male at the time he reaches puberty. If his right testicle is larger, he will give rise to male offspring; if it is the left, he will give rise to females. The same situation applies for the breasts of a girl at the time of puberty.

Chapter 24:24

A woman several months pregnant at first saw blood. After this (she saw a) rusty, dilute, foul-smelling discharge. With the passing of time, she aborted. After this, a piece of placenta was extruded every day, because the placenta had putrefied. When the remainder of the placenta was excised, the midwives and all the physicians assembled there, except myself, thought that she had been pregnant, and (her uterus) was now completely cleansed. I palpated her pulse and it became clear to me that the uterus contained a residue which was ripe to be expelled. I informed the woman and her husband of this, namely, that she would need to expel something which was still retained in the womb. It was on the sixteenth day after she aborted that a (second) fetus, that was already putrid, was aborted.

Chapter 24:29

If one excises the ovaries of a female creature, she will not lust (for coitus), and will not receive a male for pleasure.

The "power of femininity" (sex appeal?) will be abolished. Thus, female swine are castrated in the land of *Athens,* and also in other nations. Then their bodies fatten, and their flesh becomes better to eat than the flesh of other female (noncastrated) swine. If a person wishes to castrate a female, it is obligatory in this situation to remove both ovaries. In this matter the castration of a female is much more dangerous (than that of a male).

Chapter 24:30

A woman can find sexual satisfaction without a man approaching her, and this is during pollution that occurs to her during the night while she is asleep, just as this occurs to a man (at night), and after masturbation. This is just as we have related it regarding the situation of a certain woman who was a widow (in Galen's "De semine," II). This aforementioned woman is the same one whose situation is well described (at the end of Galen's "De Locis Affectis"), that is, she derived more satisfaction from illusionary sexual intercourse than actual (coitus).

Maimonides' Guide for the Perplexed

Maimonides' philosophical masterpiece entitled *Guide for the Perplexed* was composed in Arabic, and written in Hebrew characters. Subsequently it was translated into Hebrew by Rabbi Samuel Ibn Tibbon, in the lifetime of Maimonides, who was consulted by the translator on all difficult passages. The congregation in Lunel, ignorant of Ibn Tibbon's undertaking, or desirous to possess the most correct translation of the *Guide*, addressed a very flattering letter to Maimonides, requesting him to translate the work into Hebrew. Maimonides replied that he could not do so, as he had not sufficient leisure for even more pressing work, and that a translation was being prepared by the ablest and fittest man, Rabbi Samuel Ibn Tibbon. A second translation was made later on by Jehudah Alharizi. The *Guide* delighted many, but it also met with much adverse criticism on account of the peculiar views held by Maimonides concerning angels, prophecy, and miracles, especially on account of his assertion that if the Aristotelian proof for the Eternity of the Universe had satisfied him, he would have found no difficulty in reconciling the Biblical account of the Creation with that doctrine. The controversy on the *Guide* continued long after the death of Maimonides to divide the community, and it is difficult to say how far the author's hope to effect a reconciliation between reason and revelation was realized.

The purposes of the book are described by Maimonides himself in the Introduction to the work:

> My primary object in this work is to explain certain words occurring in the prophetic books. Of these some are homonyms, and of their several meanings the ignorant choose the wrong ones; other terms which are employed in a figurative sense are erroneously taken by such persons in their primary signification. There are also hybrid terms, denoting things which are of the same class from one point of view and of a different class from another. It is not here intended to explain all these expressions to the unlettered or to mere tyros, a previous knowledge of Logic and Natural Philosophy being indispensable, or to those who confine their attention to the study of our holy Law, I mean the study of the canonical law alone; for the true knowledge of the Torah is the special aim of this and similar works.
>
> The object of this treatise is to enlighten a religious man who has been trained to believe in the truth of our holy Law, who conscientiously fulfills his moral and religious duties, and at the same time has been successful in his philosophical studies. Human reason has attracted him to abide within its sphere; and he finds it difficult to accept as correct the teaching based on the literal interpretation of the Law, and especially that which he himself or others derived from those homonymous, metaphorical, or hybrid expressions. Hence he is lost in perplexity and anxiety. If he be guided solely by reason, and renounce his previous views which are based on

> those expressions, he would consider that he had rejected the fundamental principles of the Law; and even if he retains the opinions which were derived from those expressions, and if, instead of following his reason, he abandons its guidance altogether, it would still appear that his religious convictions had suffered loss and injury. For he would then be left with those errors which give rise to fear and anxiety, constant grief and great perplexity.
>
> This work has also a second object in view. It seeks to explain certain obscure figures which occur in the Prophets, and are not distinctly characterized as being figures. Ignorant and superficial readers take them in a literal, not in a figurative, sense. Even well-informed persons were bewildered if they understand these passages in their literal signification, but they are entirely relieved of their perplexity when we explain the figure, or merely suggest that the terms are figurative. For this reason I have called this book *Guide for the Perplexed.*

Maimonides wrote his *Guide for the Perplexed* in his mature age after completion of his *Mishneh Torah.* Strauss states that there is a striking difference between these two works in the method of exposition. In the *Mishneh Torah,* Maimonides sets out to produce a systematic lucid and authoritative code out of the chaotic disorder of all of Biblical and Talmudic literature, and he succeeded most admirably in this endeavor. In the *Guide,* on the other hand, expositions of Aristotelian philosophers are often disjointed and fragmented and sometimes disconnected subjects are brought together. As Maimonides explains in his introduction to the *Guide,* this was done for good and sufficient reasons and does not indicate that he had lost his expertise for lucid exposition.

A lengthy section in Part 3 of the *Guide* is concerned

with sex, lust, and morality, and is quoted below. In it, Maimonides points out that the perfect man must have complete control over his lust for food, drink and sex which impede the development of his perfection. Moderation in sex, as in all spheres of human biologic activities, is recommended by Maimonides. He points out the abhorrence in Judaism of harlotry and prostitution and the various reasons, in addition to moral repugnance, stemming from it. He further discusses the forbidden marriages in Jewish law, rather than just listing them as he does in his *Mishneh Torah* (see elsewhere in this book). Crossbreeding, intentional injury to the genitalia, adultery and other subjects relating to sex are also described and discussed from the Jewish philosophical viewpoint.

Excerpts from Maimonides' *Guide for the Perplexed*

(See M. Friedlander, *The Guide for the Perplexed by Moses Maimonides.* New York: Dover Publications, Inc., 2nd ed., 1956. LIX and 414 pp.)

Section 3, Chapter 33 (p. 327)

It is also the object of the perfect Law to make man reject, despise, and reduce his desires as much as is in his power. He should only give way to them when absolutely necessary. It is well known that it is intemperance in eating, drinking, and sexual intercourse that people mostly rave and indulge in; and these very things counteract the ulterior perfection of man, impede at the same time the development of his first perfection, and generally disturb the social order of the country and the economy of the family. For by following entirely the guidance of lust, in the manner of fools, man loses his intellectual energy, injures his body, and perishes before his natural time; sighs and cares multiply; there is an increase of envy, hatred, and warfare for the purpose of taking what another possesses. The cause of all this is the circumstance that the ignorant considers physical enjoyment as an object to be sought for its own sake. G'd in His wisdom has therefore given us such commandments as would counteract that object, and prevent us altogether from directing our attention to it, and has debarred us from everything that leads only to excessive desire and lust. This is an important thing included in the objects of our Law . . .

The Law is also intended to give its followers purity and holiness; by teaching them to suppress sensuality, to guard against it and to reduce it to a minimum, as will be explained by us. For when G-d commanded (Moses) to sanctify the people for the receiving of the Law, and said, "Sanctify them today and tomorrow" (Exod. 19:10), Moses (in obedience to this command) said to the people, "Come not at your wives" (*ibid.* ver. 15). Here it is clearly stated that sanctification consists in absence of sensuality . . .

Cleanliness in dress and body by washing and removing sweat and dirt is included among the various objects of the Law, but only if connected with purity of action, and with a heart free from low principles and bad habits. It would be extremely bad for man to content himself with a purity obtained by washing and cleanliness in dress, and to be at the same time voluptuous and unrestrained in food and lust. These are described by Isaiah as follows: "They that sanctify themselves and purify themselves in the gardens, but continue their sinful life, when they are in the innermost (of their houses), eating swine's flesh, and the abomination, and the mouse" (Isaiah 67): that is to say, they purify and sanctify themselves outwardly as much as is exposed to the sight of the people, and when they are alone in their chambers and the inner parts of their houses, they continue their rebelliousness and disobedience, and indulge in partaking of forbidden food, such as (the flesh of) swine, worms, and mice. The prophet alludes perhaps in the phrase "behind one tree in the midst" to indulgence in forbidden lust. The sense of the passage is therefore this: they appear outwardly clean, but their heart is bent upon their desires and bodily enjoyments, and this is contrary to the spirit of the Law. For the chief object of the Law is to (teach man to) diminish his desires, and to cleanse his outer appearance after he has purified his heart. Those who wash their body and cleanse their garments whilst they remain dirty by bad actions and principles, are described by Solomon as "a generation that are pure in their own eyes, and yet are not washed from their filthiness; a generation, oh how lofty are their eyes!" etc. (Prov. 30: 12–13). Consider well the principles which we mentioned in this chapter as the final causes of the Law; for there are many precepts, for which you will be unable to give a reason unless you possess a knowledge of these principles, as will be explained further on.

Section 3, Chapter 49 (p. 372)

. . . It is well known that man requires friends all his lifetime. Aristotle explains this in the ninth book of his Nikomachean Ethics. When man is in good health and prosperous, he enjoys the company of his friends; in time of trouble he is in need of them; in old age, when his body is weak, he is assisted by them. This love is more frequent and more intense between parents and children, and among (other) relations. Perfect love, brotherhood, and mutual assistance is only found among those near to each other by relationship. The members of a family united by common descent from the same grandfather, or even from some more distant ancestor, have towards each other a certain feeling of love, help each other, and sympathize with each other. To effect this is one of the chief purposes of the Law. Professional harlots were therefore not tolerated in Israel (Deut. 23:18), because their existence would disturb the above relationship between man and man. Their children are strangers to everybody; no one knows to what family they belong; nor does any person recognize them as relatives. And this is the greatest misfortune that can befall any child or father. Another important object in prohibiting prostitution is to restrain excessive and continual lust; for lust increases with the variety of its objects. The sight of that to which a person has been accustomed for a long time does not produce such an ardent desire for its enjoyment as is produced by objects new in form and character. Another effect of this prohibition is the removal of a cause for strife; for if the prohibition did not exist, several persons might by chance come to one woman, and would naturally quarrel with each other; they would in many cases kill one another, or they would kill the woman. This is known to have occurred in days of old, "And they assembled themselves by troops in a harlot's house" (Jer. 5:7). In order to prevent these great evils, and to effect the great boon that all men should know their relationship to each other, prostitutes (Deut. 23:17) were not tolerated, and sexual intercourse was only permitted when man has chosen a certain female, and married her openly; for if it sufficed merely to choose her, many a person would bring a prostitute into his house at a certain time agreed upon between them, and say that she was his wife. Therefore it is commanded to perform the act of engagement by which he declares that he has chosen her to take her for his wife, and then to go through the public ceremony of marriage. Comp. "And Boaz took ten men," etc. (Ruth 4:2). It may happen that husband

and wife do not agree, live without love and peace, and do not enjoy the benefit of a home; in that case he is permitted to send her away. If he had been allowed to divorce her by a mere word, or by turning her out of his house, the wife would wait for some negligence (on the part of the husband), and then come out and say that she was divorced; or having committed adultery, she and the adulterer would contend that she had then been divorced. Therefore the law is that divorce can only take place by means of a document which can serve as evidence, "He shall write her a bill of divorcement" (Deut. 24:1). There are frequently occasions for suspicion of adultery and doubts concerning the conduct of the wife. Laws concerning a wife suspected of adultery *(sotah)* are therefore prescribed (Numb.5); the effect of which is that the wife, out of fear of the "bitter waters," is most careful to prevent any ill-feeling on the part of her husband against her. Even of those that felt quite innocent and safe, most were rather willing to lose all their property than to submit to the prescribed treatment; even death was preferred to the public disgrace of uncovering the head, undoing the hair, rending the garments and exposing the heart, and being led around through the Sanctuary in the presence of all, of women and men, and also in the presence of the members of the *Synhedrion.* The fear of this trial keeps away great diseases that ruin the home comfort.

As every maiden expects to be married, her seducer therefore is only ordered to marry her; for he is undoubtedly the fittest husband for her. He will better heal her wound and redeem her character than any other husband. If, however, he is rejected by her or her father, he must give the dowry (Exod. 22:15). If he uses violence he has to submit to the additional punishment, "he may not put her away all his days (Deut. 22:29).

The reason of the law concerning marrying the deceased

brother's wife is stated in the Bible (Deut. 25:5). It was a custom in force before the Law was given and the Law perpetuated it . . .

The law about forbidden sexual intercourse seeks in all its parts to inculcate the lesson that we ought to limit sexual intercourse altogether, hold it in contempt, and only desire it very rarely. The prohibition of pederasty (Lev.18:22) and carnal intercourse with beasts (*ibid.* 23) is very clear. If in the natural way the act is too base to be performed except when needed, how much more base is it if performed in an unnatural manner, and only for the sake of pleasure.

The female relatives whom a man may not marry are alike in this respect—that as a rule they are constantly together with him in his house; they would easily listen to him, and do what he desires; they are near at hand, and he would have no difficulty in procuring them. No judge could blame him if found in their company. If to these relatives the same law applied as to all other unmarried women, if we were allowed to marry any of them, and were only precluded from sexual intercourse with them without marriage, most people would constantly have become guilty of misconduct with them. But as they are entirely forbidden to us, and sexual intercourse with them is most emphatically denounced unto us as a capital crime, or a sin punishable with extinction *(karet)*, and as there is no means of ever legalizing such intercourse, there is reason to expect that people will not seek it, and will not think of it. That the persons included in that prohibition are, as we have stated, at hand and easily accessible is evident. For as a rule, the mother of the wife, the grandmother, the daughter, the granddaughter, and the sister-in-law are mostly with her; the husband meets them always when he goes out, when he comes in, and when he is at his work. The wife stays also frequently in the house of her husband's brother, father, or son. It is also well known that we are often in the company of our sisters, our aunts, and the wife of our uncle, and are frequently brought up together with them. These are all the relatives whom we must not marry. This is one of the reasons why intermarriage with a near relative is forbidden. But according to my opinion the prohibition serves another object, namely, to inculcate chastity into our hearts. License between the root and the branch, between a man and his mother or his daughter, is outrageous. The intercourse between root and branch is forbidden, and it makes no difference whether the male element is the root or the branch, or both root and branch combine in the intercourse with a third person, so that the same individual cohabits with the root and with the branch. On this account it is prohibited to marry a woman and her mother, the wife of the father or of the son; for in all these cases there is the intercourse between one and the same person on the one side and root and branch on the other.

The law concerning brothers is like the law concerning root and branch. The sister is forbidden, and so is also the sister of the wife and the wife of the brother; because in the latter cases two persons who are considered like root and branch cohabit with the same person. But in these prohibitions brothers and sisters are partly considered as root and branch and partly as one body; the sister of the mother is therefore like the mother, and the sister of the father like the father, and both are prohibited; and since the daughter of the parent's brother or sister is not included in the number of prohibited relatives, so may we also marry the daughter of the brother or the sister. The apparent anomaly, that the brother of the father may marry a woman that has been the wife of his brother's son, whilst the nephew must not marry a woman that has been the wife of his father's brother, can be explained according to the above-mentioned first reason. For the nephew is frequently in the house of his uncle, and his conduct towards the wife of his uncle is the same as that towards his brother's wife. The uncle, however, is not so frequent in the house of his nephew, and he is consequently less intimate with the wife of his nephew; whilst in the case of father and son, the familiarity of the father with his daughter-in-law is the same as that of the son with the wife of his father, and therefore the law and punishment is the same for both (father and son). The reason why it is prohibited to cohabit with a menstruous woman (Lev. 18:19) or with another man's wife (*ibid.* 20), is obvious, and requires no further explanation.

It is well known that we must not indulge in any sensual enjoyment whatever with the persons included in the above prohibitions; we must not even look at them if we intend to derive pleasure therefrom. We have explained this in "the laws about forbidden sexual intercourse" (*Hilkot issure biyah*, 21: 1–2), and shown that according to the Law we must not even engage our thoughts with the act of cohabitation (*ibid.* 19) or irritate the organ of generation; and when we find ourselves unintentionally in a state of irritation, we must turn our mind to other thoughts, and reflect on some other thing till we are relieved. Our Sages (B.T. *Kidd* 30b), in their moral lessons, which give perfection to the virtuous, say as follows: "My son, if that monster meets you, drag it to the house of study. It will melt if it is of iron; it will break in pieces if it is of stone: as is said in Scripture, 'Is not my word like a fire? saith the Lord, and like a hammer that breaketh the rock in pieces?' " (Jer. 23:29). The author of this saying thus exhorts his son to go to the house of study when he finds his organ of generation in an irritated state. By reading, disputing, asking, and listening to questions, the irritation will certainly cease. See how properly the term "monster" is employed, for that irritation is indeed like a monster. Not only religion teaches this lesson, the philosophers teach the same.

I have already quoted verbatim the words of Aristotle. He says: "The sense of touch which is a disgrace to us, leads us to indulge in eating and sensuality," etc. He calls people degraded who seek carnal pleasures and devote themselves to gastronomy; he denounces *in extenso* their low and objectionable conduct, and ridicules them. This passage occurs in his *Ethics* and in his *Rhetoric.*

In accordance with this excellent principle, which we ought strictly to follow, our Sages teach us that we ought not to look at beasts or birds in the moment of the copulation. According to my opinion, this is the reason why the crossbreeding of cattle is prohibited (Lev. 19:19). It is a fact that animals of different species do not copulate together, unless by force. It is well known that the low class of breeders of mules are regularly engaged in this work. Our Law objected to it that any Israelite should degrade himself by doing these things, which require so much vulgarity and indecency, and doing that which religion forbids us even to mention, how much more to witness or to practice, except when necessary. Crossbreeding, however, is not necessary. I think that the prohibition to bring together two species in any kind of work, as included in the words, "Thou shalt not plow with an ox and an ass together" (Deut. 22:10), is only a preventive against the intercourse of two species. For if it were allowed to join such together in any work, we might sometimes also cause their intercourse. That this is the reason of the commandment is proved by the fact that it applies to other animals besides ox and ass; it is prohibited to plow not only with ox and ass together, but with any two kinds. But Scripture mentions as an instance that which is of regular occurrence. . . .

As regards circumcision, I think that one of its objects is to limit sexual intercourse, and to weaken the organ of generation as far as possible, and thus cause man to be moderate. Some people believe that circumcision is to remove a defect in man's formation; but everyone can easily reply: How can products of nature be deficient so as to require external completion, especially as the use of the foreskin to that organ is evident. This commandment has not been enjoined as a complement to a deficient physical creation, but as a means for perfecting man's moral shortcomings. The bodily injury caused to that organ is exactly that which is desired; it does not interrupt any vital function, nor does it destroy the power of generation. Circumcision simply counteracts excessive lust; for there is no doubt that circumcision weakens the power of sexual excitement, and sometimes lessens the natural enjoyment; the organ necessarily becomes weak when it loses blood and is deprived of its covering from the beginning. Our Sages (Beresh. Rabba, c.80) say distinctly: It is hard for a woman, with whom an uncircumcised had sexual intercourse, to separate from him. This is, as I believe, the best reason for the commandment concerning circumcision. And who was the first to perform this commandment? Abraham, our father! of whom it is well known how he feared sin; it is described by our Sages in reference to the words, "Behold, now I know that thou art a fair woman to look upon" (Gen. 12:2).

There is, however, another important object in this commandment. It gives to all members of the same faith, i.e., to all believers in the Unity of God, a common bodily sign, so that it is impossible for anyone that is a stranger to say that he belongs to them. For sometimes people say so for the purpose of obtaining some advantage, or in order to make some attack upon the Jews. No one, however, should circumcise himself or his son for any other reason but pure faith; for circumcision is not like an incision on the leg, or a burning in the arm, but a very difficult operation. It is also a fact that there is much mutual love and assistance among people that are united by the same sign when they consider it as [symbol of the] covenant which Abraham made in connection with the belief in God's Unity. So also every one that is circumcised enters the covenant of Abraham to believe in the unity of God, in accordance with the words of the Law, "To be a God unto thee, and to thy seed after thee" (Gen. 17:7). This purpose of the circumcision is as important as the first, and perhaps more important.

This law can only be kept and perpetuated in its perfection, if circumcision is performed when the child is very young, and this for three good reasons. First, if the operation were postponed till the boy had grown up, he would perhaps not submit to it. Secondly, the young child has not much pain, because the skin is tender, and the imagination weak; for grown-up persons are in dread and fear of things which they imagine as coming, some time before these actually occur. Thirdly, when a child is very young, the parents do not think much of him; because the image of the child, that leads the parents to love him, has not yet taken a firm root in their minds. That image becomes stronger by the continual sight; it grows with the development of the child, and later on the image begins again to decrease and to vanish. The parents' love for a newborn child is not so great as it is when the child is one year old; and when one year old, it is less loved by them than when six years old. The feeling and love of the father for the child would have led him to neglect the law if he were allowed to wait two or three years, whilst shortly after birth the image is very weak in the mind of the parent, especially of the father who is responsible for the execution of this commandment. The circumcision must take place on the eighth day (Lev. 12:3), because all living beings are after birth, within the first seven days, very weak and exceedingly tender, as if they were still in the womb of their mother; not until the eighth day can they be counted among those that enjoy the light of the world. That this is also the case with beasts may be inferred from the words of Scripture: "Seven days shall it be under the dam" (Lev. 22:27), as if it had no vitality before the end of that period. In the same manner man is circumcised after the completion of seven days. The period has been fixed, and has not been left to everybody's judgment.

The precepts of this class include also the lesson that we must not injure in any way the organs of generation in living beings (Levit. 22:24). The lesson is based on the principle of "righteous statutes and judgments" (Deut. 4:8); we must keep in everything the golden mean; we must not be excessive in love, but must not suppress it entirely; for the Law commands, "Be fruitful, and multiply" (Gen. 1:22). The organ is weakened by circumcision, but not destroyed by the operation. The natural faculty is left in full force, but is guarded against excess. It is prohibited for an Israelite "that is wounded in the stones, or hath his privy member cut off" (Deut. 23:2), to marry an Israelitish woman; because the sexual intercourse is of no use and of no purpose; and that marriage would be a source of ruin to her, and to him who would claim her. This is very clear.

In order to create a horror of illicit marriages, a bastard was not allowed to marry an Israelitish woman (*ibid.* 23:3); the adulterer and the adulteress were thus taught that by their act they bring upon their seed irreparable injury. In every language and in every nation the issue of licentious conduct has a bad name; the Law therefore raises the name of the Israelites by keeping them free from the admixture of bastards. The priests, who have a higher sanctity, are not allowed to marry a harlot or a woman that is divorced from her husband, or that is profane (Lev. 21:7); the high priest, the noblest of the priests, must not marry even a widow, or a woman that has had sexual intercourse of any kind (*ibid.* 21:14).

Maimonides' Book of Holiness

The subject of forbidden marriages in Judaism is described by Rabbi J. H. Hertz in his commentary on Leviticus. Briefly, all unions between the sexes that are repellent to the moral inner feelings of man, or would taint the natural affection between close relatives, are strictly prohibited. Such prohibited marriages and illicit sexual intercourse comprise two major categories: firstly, blood relations such as mother, sister, daughter, granddaughter, father's sister and mother's sister; and secondly, cases of affinity such as the wives of blood relations and of the wife's blood relations.

All sexual unions, whether temporary or permanent, between persons belonging to these groups are called incestuous and hence prohibited and abhorrent. They have no binding force whatsoever in Jewish law and can in no circumstance be deemed a marriage. Hence, no bill of divorce is required for their dissolution and the children which issue from such a union are illegitimate.

The Sages of Judaism expanded the primary prohibited

degrees of illicit marriages in the ascending and descending line. These expansions are known as secondary prohibited marriages. For example, as the mother is forbidden, so is the grandmother and great-grandmother; as the stepmother is forbidden, so is the grandfather's wife; as the daughter-in-law is forbidden, so is the grandson's wife. Marriages of the secondary prohibited degrees must be dissolved by a bill of divorce, and the children are legitimate.

These prohibited marriages and prohibited degrees of marriage, whether Biblical or Rabbinical, are based on instructive abhorrence and natural decorum. Prior to the Revelation at Sinai, only the following marriages were prohibited: mother, father's wife, a married woman, and sister on the mother's side. Hence, concludes Hertz, Abraham was permitted to marry his half-sister, and Jacob two sisters.

There was a dire need for the Mosaic Code to prohibit such incestuous marriages, which were not unusual in antiquity and were recognized in parts of the Roman world as late as the early Middle Ages. In ancient Egypt, marriage with a sister was common practice, especially in the royal families. The Greeks countenanced marriage with a half-sister. Among the Persians, marriages with mothers, sisters and daughters were expressly recommended as meritorious and as most pleasing to their gods. These were practices not of pagan and barbarian tribes but of the cultured nations of antiquity. Hence, the influence of the Mosaic Code prohibiting such incestuous marriages on the Western and Near Eastern peoples has indeed been very significant.

The *Book of Holiness* of Maimonides' *Mishneh Torah,* or Code, also contains discussions of such subjects as sodomy, homosexuality, lesbianism, masturbation, onanism, rape, bestiality, incest, adultery, menstruation. Furthermore, the time and place and quantity of sexual intercourse which are desirable according to the Torah are described. Excerpts from this book of Maimonides' Code follow the listing of prohibited marriages and cohabitations.

Laws Concerning Illicit Intercourse

(See L.I. Rabinowitz and P. Grossman, *The Code of Maimonides.* Book Five: The Book of Holiness. New Haven: Yale Univ. Press, 1965. XXXIV and 429 pp.)

Note:

The fifth book of Maimonides' great codification of ancient Jewish law and ritual sets forth the rule and exercise of holy living as prescribed by divine ordinance. To be holy, man must forgo sensual excess. Maimonides stresses the disciplinary intent of the laws, which counteract the worldly tendency to regard pleasure as the purpose of man's existence. Chastity and temperance are seen as higher disciplines. The path to holy living, shown by the Law, lies through self-disciplined abstention from that which is characteristically bestial, and wholehearted practice of that which is characteristically divine. There follows below the introductory section to this fifth book of the Maimonides' Code which is an outline of the entire contents of the book. For more details, the interested reader is referred to the main text of the book itself either in the original Hebrew, or in the English translation listed above.

Laws Concerning Forbidden Intercourse

Involving Thirty-Seven Commandments,
One Positive and Thirty-Six Negative
To Wit

1. Not to have intercourse with one's mother;
2. Not to have intercourse with the wife of one's father;
3. Not to cohabit with one's sister;
4. Not to cohabit with the daughter of the wife of one's father;
5. Not to cohabit with the daughter of one's son;
6. Not to cohabit with one's daughter;
7. Not to cohabit with the daughter of one's daughter;
8. Not to marry a woman and her daughter;
9. Not to marry a woman and her son's daughter;
10. Not to marry a woman and her daughter's daughter;
11. Not to cohabit with the sister of one's father;
12. Not to cohabit with the sister of one's mother;
13. Not to cohabit with the wife of one's father's brother;
14. Not to cohabit with the wife of one's son;
15. Not to cohabit with the wife of one's brother;
16. Not to cohabit with the sister of one's wife;
17. Not to lie with an animal;
18. That a woman should not cause an animal to go in unto her;
19. Not to lie with a male;
20. Not to uncover the nakedness of one's father;
21. Not to uncover the nakedness of the brother of one's father;

22. Not to cohabit with a married woman;
23. Not to cohabit with a menstruant;
24. Not to intermarry with heathens;
25. That an Ammonite or Moabite shall not be permitted to enter the congregation of the Lord;
26. Not to repulse an Egyptian proselyte of the third generation from entering the congregation of the Lord;
27. Not to repulse an Edomite proselyte of the third generation from entering the congregation of the Lord;
28. That a bastard shall not be permitted to enter the congregation of the Lord;
29. That a eunuch shall not be permitted to enter the congregation of the Lord;
30. Not to castrate a male, even of animal, beast, or bird;
31. That a High Priest shall not marry a widow;
32. That a High Priest shall not cohabit with a widow, even out of wedlock;
33. That a High Priest shall marry only a virgin during her maidenhood;
34. That a priest shall not marry a divorced woman;
35. That he shall not marry a harlot;
36. That he shall not marry a profaned woman;
37. Not to approach lasciviously any of the women within the forbidden degrees of consanguinity, even if one has no intercourse with her.

An exposition of these commandments is contained in the following chapters.

Chapter 1:

14. In the case of a man who lies with a male, or causes a male to have connection with him, once sexual contact has been initiated, the rule is as follows: If both are adults, they are punishable by stoning, as it is said, *Thou*

shalt not lie with a male (Lev. 18:22), i.e., whether he is the active or the passive participant in the act. If he is a minor, aged nine years and one day, or older, the adult who has connection with him or causes him to have connection with him, is punishable by stoning, while the minor is exempt. If the minor is nine years old, or less, both are exempt. It behooves the court, however, to have the adult flogged for disobedience, inasmuch as he has lain with a male, even though with one less than nine years of age.

15. If one has connection with a hermaphrodite by way of the latter's male organ, he is liable; if by way of the latter's female organ, he is exempt. A *tumtum*, however, is of doubtful sex, and consequently if one has intercourse with him, or with a hermaphrodite by way of the latter's female organ, he must be flogged for disobedience. A hermaphrodite is nevertheless permitted to take a wife.

16. If a man has connection with an animal, or causes an animal to have connection with him, both are punishable by stoning, as it is said, *And thou shalt not lie with any beast* (Lev. 18:23), i.e., whether he is the active or passive participant in the act. Regardless of whether it is a domestic animal, a wild beast, or a fowl, in all these cases the penalty is death by stoning. Nor does Scripture differentiate between a fully grown animal and one not yet fully grown, seeing that it is said *any beast,* i.e., even a newly born beast. Whether he has connection in a natural manner or not, once he has initiated sexual contact with it, or has caused it to initiate contact with him, he is liable.

Chapter 21:

1. Whosoever has intercourse with a woman within the forbidden unions, whether by way of the sexual organs, or by way of lustful embracing or kissing, thus deriving pleasure from carnal proximity, is liable to a flogging on the authority of the Torah, as it is said, *that ye do not any of these abominable customs* (Lev. 18:30), and it is also said, *none of you shall approach to any that is near of kin to him to uncover their nakedness* (*ibid.* 18:6); that is to say, you shall not even approach things which lead to forbidden union.
2. Whosoever indulges in these practices lays himself open to the suspicion of forbidden unions. A man is forbidden to make suggestive gestures with his hands or legs or to wink at a woman within the forbidden unions, or to jest or act frivolously with her. It is forbidden even to inhale her perfume or gaze at her beauty. Whosoever directs his mind towards these things is liable to the flogging prescribed for disobedience. He who stares even at a woman's little finger with the intention of deriving pleasure from it is considered as though he had looked at her secret parts. It is forbidden even to listen to the singing of a woman within the forbidden unions, or to look at her hair.
3. These things are forbidden with regard to a woman prohibited to a man by a negative commandment; on the other hand, he is permitted to look at an unmarried woman, whether she is a virgin or not, and to inspect her, so that if she is pleasing in his sight he may marry her. Not only is there no suggestion of prohibition about this, but it is indeed proper to do so. He should not, however, look at her adulterously, for Scripture says, *I*

made a covenant with mine eyes, how then should I look upon a maiden? (Job 31:1).

4. A man is permitted to look at his wife while she is a menstruant, even though she is forbidden to him at that time. For while his heart will be pleased by the sight of her, nevertheless, seeing that she will become permitted to him after her menstruation, he will not be led now to temptation thereby. But he should not jest or act frivolously with her, lest he should become addicted to transgression.
5. The services of a woman are utterly forbidden to a man, whether she is an adult or a minor, a bondswoman or a manumitted woman, lest he should come thereby to sinful thoughts. What services are here referred to? Washing his face, hands, or feet, arranging his bed in his presence, and pouring his wine, since only his own wife should perform these duties for him. A man may not inquire after the well-being of a woman at all, not even through a messenger.
6. If a man innocently embraces or kisses a woman within the forbidden unions—for instance, his elder sister, maternal aunt, or the like—even though neither lust nor pleasure is involved in the act at all, it is nevertheless most disgraceful, and is forbidden, being the act of a fool. For a man should not come nigh to a woman forbidden to him under any circumstances, whether she is an adult or a minor; the sole exceptions are a mother with her son, and a father with his daughter.
7. How so? A father is permitted to embrace and kiss his daughter, and she may sleep with him with their bodies touching, and similarly a mother with her son, while the children are minors. When they come of age, the son reaching his majority, and the daughter developing firm breasts and a growth of hair, he must then sleep in his

clothes, and she in hers. If the daughter feels ashamed to stand naked before her father, or if she is married, or similarly, if the mother is ashamed to stand naked in the presence of her son, even though they are minors, once they have reached the stage of feeling shame, they must sleep together only in their clothes.

8. Women are forbidden to engage in lesbian practices with one another, these being *the doings of the land of Egypt* (Lev. 18:3), against which we have been warned, as it is said, *After the doings of the land of Egypt . . . ye shall not do (ibid).* Our Sages have said, "What did they do? A man would marry a man, or a woman a woman, or a woman would marry two men." Although such an act is forbidden, the perpetrators are not liable to a flogging, since there is no specific negative commandment prohibiting it, nor is actual intercourse of any kind involved here. Consequently, such women are not forbidden for the priesthood on account of harlotry, nor is a woman prohibited to her husband because of it, since this does not constitute harlotry. It behooves the court, however, to administer the flogging prescribed for disobedience, since they have performed a forbidden act. A man should be particularly strict with his wife in this matter, and should prevent women known to indulge in such practices from visiting her, and her from going to visit them.

9. Since a man's wife is permitted to him, he may act with her in any manner whatsoever. He may have intercourse with her whenever he so desires, and kiss any organ of her body he wishes, and he may have intercourse with her naturally or unnaturally, provided that he does not expend semen to no purpose. Nevertheless, it is an attribute of piety that a man should not act in this matter with levity and that he should sanctify himself at

the time of intercourse, as we have explained in the Laws Concerning Knowledge. A man should not turn aside from the normal way of the world and its proper procedure, since the true design of intercourse is fruitfulness and multiplication of progeny.

10. A man is forbidden to have intercourse by the light of a lamp. If it is Sabbath, and he has no other room than the one in which a light is burning, he should abstain from intercourse entirely. Similarly, an Israelite is forbidden to have intercourse during daylight, since this constitutes shameless behavior. If he is a scholar, who would not be likely to make it a habit, he may envelop himself in darkness by spreading his cloak over himself and then have intercourse. But he should not have recourse to this expedient except in case of great need, and the way of sanctity is to have intercourse in the middle of the night only.

11. The Sages have found no pleasure in the man who indulges in sexual intercourse to excess and is as frequently with his wife as a cock is with his hen. Such conduct is a serious blemish, and brands him as a boor. The more continent a man is, the more is he praiseworthy, provided he does not neglect his marital duty without his wife's consent. Indeed, the original reason why the rule was enacted that a man who had a nocturnal pollution should not read in the Torah before immersing himself was in order to reduce sexual intercourse.

12. Similarly, the Sages have forbidden a man to have intercourse with his wife while thinking in his heart of another woman. Nor should he have intercourse while intoxicated or in the midst of strife or hatred. Nor should he have intercourse with her against her will while she is in dread of him, nor when one of them is

under a ban, nor after he has made up his mind to divorce her. If he does one of these things, the resulting children will be degenerate; some will be shameless, others will become renegades and sinners.

13. Similarly, the Sages have said that in the case of a woman who is so barefaced as to brazenly demand intercourse, or seduces a man in order to make him marry her, or persuades her husband to have intercourse with her when his intention is to visit his other wife, or does not wait three months after the death of her husband before remarrying—with the result that the parentage of the resulting child is in doubt—all children born of such women become renegades and sinners who become separated in the sufferings of exile.
14. A man is forbidden to have intercourse with his wife in public places and streets, or in gardens and orchards; he may have it only in their dwelling, so that it should not seem like harlotry and thus cause them to accustom themselves to harlotry. If a man has intercourse with his wife in such places, he should be given the flogging prescribed for disobedience. Similarly, he who betrothes his wife by an act of intercourse, or in the marketplace, or without proper negotiation, is also liable to the flogging prescribed for disobedience.
15. A guest staying at an inn is forbidden to have intercourse with his wife until he returns home. Similarly, the Sages have forbidden a man to reside in the house of his father-in-law, since this constitutes shamelessness; nor should he enter a bathhouse with him.
16. Nor should a man enter a bathhouse with his father or with his sister's husband, or with his disciple. If, however, he has need of his disciple's services in the bath, it is permitted. There are localities where custom forbids two brothers to enter a bathhouse together.

17. Daughters of Israel should not walk in the marketplace bareheaded, regardless of whether they are unmarried or married, nor should a woman walk in the marketplace with her son following behind her, lest he should be seized and she should then pursue in order to retrieve him, and the rogues who had originally seized the boy for mere sport would thereupon ravish her.
18. It is forbidden to expend semen to no purpose. Consequently, a man should not thresh within and ejaculate without, nor should a man marry a minor who cannot yet bear children. As for masturbators, not only do they commit a strictly forbidden act, but they also expose themselves to a ban. It is to them that Scripture refers in saying, *Your hands are full of blood* (Isa. 1:15), and a masturbator's act is regarded as equivalent to killing a human being.
19. Similarly, a man is forbidden to bring about an erection or unchaste thoughts deliberately. If such thoughts do enter his mind, he should direct it away from thoughts of vanity leading to wastage of semen, and back to words of Torah, which is a *hind of love and a doe of grace* (Prov. 5:19). A man is therefore forbidden to sleep on his back, face upwards, unless he inclines a little to one side, in order not to bring about an erection.
20. Nor should he look at domestic animals, wild beasts, or birds when male and female are mating. Animal breeders, however, are permitted to insert the male organ into the female, for inasmuch as they are absorbed in their work they are not likely to think of lustful matters.
21. Similarly, a man is forbidden to gaze upon women while they are bending over their washing, and he is even forbidden to look at the brightly colored clothes belonging to a woman whom he knows, lest indecent thoughts should enter his mind.

22. If a man meets a woman in the street, he is forbidden to walk behind her, and should hasten on so as to have her walk by his side or behind him. Whosoever walks in the street behind a woman is considered a most worthless boor. A man is forbidden to pass by a harlot's door unless he keeps a distance of four cubits from it, as it is said, *and come not nigh the door of her house* (Prov. 5:8).
23. An unmarried man is forbidden to take hold of his privy parts, lest this should cause unchaste thoughts. He should not even insert his hand below the navel, for the same reason. When he urinates, he should not hold his organ, but if he is married, he may do so. Whether he is married or not, he should never put his hand to his organ, except when relieving himself.
24. One of the early pietists and most distinguished Sages prided himself on the fact that he had never in his life looked upon his circumcision, while another stated with pride that he had never looked upon his wife's figure, for his thoughts were always turned away from matters of vanity toward those of truth which take hold of the hearts of saintly men.
25. It is an injunction of the Sages that a man should marry off his sons and daughters as near to puberty as possible, for if he leaves them unmarried they will be led to adultery or to indecent thoughts, and concerning this it is said, *and thou shalt think of thy habitation, and not sin* (Job 5:24). It is also forbidden to marry an adult woman to a minor, since this is considered the same as harlotry.
26. A man is not permitted to live without a wife, nor should he marry a barren woman or a woman too old for childbearing; a woman, on the other hand, has the right to remain unmarried or to marry a eunuch. A young man

should not marry an old woman, nor an old man a young girl, since this leads to harlotry.

27. Similarly, a man who has divorced his wife after marriage should not reside with her in the same courtyard, lest they should come to adultery; if he is a priest, she should not reside even in the same alley with him. A small village is regarded in this respect as equivalent to an alley. If he owes her money, she should appoint an agent to demand repayment. If a divorced woman comes to court for a lawsuit with her divorced husband, they both should be put under a ban or be given the flogging prescribed for disobedience. If she had been divorced after betrothal, she is permitted to summon him to a lawsuit and dwell in the same courtyard, but if he is on terms of familiarity with her, she is forbidden to do so even if the divorce followed betrothal. Which one must give way? She must give way to him, but if the courtyard is her own property, he must give way to her.
28. A man is forbidden to marry a woman with the intention of subsequently divorcing her, as it is said, *Devise not evil against thy neighbor while he dwelleth securely by thee* (Prov. 3:29). If, however, he informs her at the outset that he is marrying her only for a specified period, it is permitted.
29. A man should not marry one wife in one country and another in another country, lest with the passage of time it should happen that his son would marry his own sister, or his mother's or father's sister, or the like, without being aware of it. If, however, the father is a distinguished man whose name is well known and whose children would therefore also be widely and well known, it is permitted.
30. A man should not marry a woman belonging to a family of lepers or epileptics, provided that there is a presump-

tion based on three cases that the disease is hereditary with them.

31. If a woman had been successively married to two husbands and both died, she should not marry for a third time, but if she does so, she need not be divorced. Even if only the betrothal has taken place, the third husband may consummate the marriage. An unlettered Israelite should not marry a woman of priestly descent, since this constitutes in a way a profanation of the seed of Aaron. Should he marry her nevertheless, the Sages have said that the marriage will not prove successful, and he will die childless, or else he or she will come to an early death, or there will be strife between them. On the other hand, it is laudable and praiseworthy for a scholar to marry a woman of priestly descent, since in this instance learning and priesthood are united.
32. A man should not marry the daughter of an unlettered person, for if he should die or be sent into exile, his children would grow up in ignorance, since their mother knows not of the crown of the Torah. Nor should a man marry his daughter to an unlettered person, for one who gives his daughter in marriage to such a husband is as though he had bound her and placed her in front of a lion, seeing that the beast's habit is to smite his mate and have intercourse with her, since he has no shame. A man should go so far as to sell all his possessions in order to marry a scholar's daughter, for should he die or go into exile, his children would grow up to be scholars. Similarly, he should marry his daughter to a scholar, since there is no reprehensible thing or strife in the house of a scholar.

Chapter 22:

18. There is no prohibition in the whole of Scripture which the generality of the people experience greater diffi-

culty in observing than the interdict of forbidden unions and illicit intercourse. The Sages have declared that when Israel was given the commandments concerning forbidden unions, they wept and accepted this injunction with grumbling and wailing, as it is said, *weeping in their families* (Num. 11:10), i.e., weeping on account of the matter of family relations.

19. The Sages have declared further that the soul of man lusts after larceny and forbidden unions and covets them. At no time can one find a community which does not contain libertines indulging in forbidden unions and illicit intercourse. And the Sages have declared also, "The majority of men are guilty of larceny, the minority of forbidden unions, and all of them together of the tendency to evil tongue."

20. Consequently, it behooves a man to subdue his inclination towards these vices and to inure himself to unbounded sanctity, pure thought, and disciplined moral disposition, so as to be saved from such transgressions. Above all, he should be on guard against improper seclusion, since this is the chief contributory factor to unchastity. The greatest of our Sages used to say to their disciples, "Warn me to beware of my daughter, warn me to beware of my daughter-in-law," in order to teach their disciples not to feel embarrassed in such matters and to keep away from improper seclusion.

21. In like manner, man should keep away from levity, drunkenness, and lewd discourse, since these are great contributory factors and degrees leading to forbidden unions. Nor should a man live without a wife, since married estate is conducive to great purity. But above all this, as the Sages have declared, a man should direct his mind and thoughts to the words of Torah and enlarge his understanding with wisdom, for unchaste

thoughts prevail only in a heart devoid of wisdom, and of wisdom it is said, *a hind of love and a doe of grace, let her breasts satisfy thee at all times, with her love be thou ravished always* (Prov. 5:19).

Maimonides' Book of Women

In the *Book of Women,* Maimonides discusses laws of marriage, divorce, levirate marriage, the virgin maiden and the wayward woman. A variety of subjects are covered in this book of Maimonides' Code including seduction, rape, infidelity, marriage eligibility, polygamy, childhood marriages, physical signs of puberty, hermaphrodites, eunuchs, wedding procedures, conjugal rights and obligations, duty of propagation, impotence, sterility and many others. Only a few brief excerpts are presented here. The interested reader can consult the original, which is now available in English.

Excerpts from the Code of Maimonides' Book of Women

(See I. Klein, *The Code of Maimonides.* Book Four: The Book of Women. New Haven: Yale Univ. Press, 1972. XXXVII and 506 pp.)

Treatise 1; Chapter 1:1

Before the revelation of the Torah, when a man would encounter a woman in the street, if both consented to marriage, he would bring her into his house and would have intercourse with her in privacy, and thereby she would become his wife.

Upon the revelation of the Torah, the people of Israel were commanded that if a man wishes to marry a woman, he must first acquire her in the presence of witnesses, and only thereafter does she become his wife, as it is said: *If any man take a wife and go in unto her* (Deut. 22:13).

Chapter 1:4

Before the revelation of the Torah, when a man would encounter a woman in the street, if both were willing, he would pay her her fee, have intercourse with her right there at the crossroads, and go his way. Such a woman is called a harlot.

Upon the revelation of the Torah, harlots were forbidden, as it is said: *There shall be no harlot of the daughters of Israel* (Deut. 23:18).

Treatise 4; Chapter 1:1

He who seduces a virgin must be fined the weight of fifty *sela* of refined silver. This is called a "fine" (*kenas*). The same applies to one who violates a virgin. . . .

Chapter 1:2

Who is a seducer, and who is a violator? A seducer acts with the victim's consent; a violator has intercourse with her against her will. . . .

Maimonides' Commentary on the Mishnah

Maimonides' first major work is his *Commentary on the Mishnah*, which he completed at age thirty-three, in the year 1168, shortly after settling in Fostat (old Cairo). This work, as the name indicates, represents Maimonides' commentary on the sixty-three tractates of *Mishnah*. In the fourth *Mishnah* of Chapter 7 of Tractate Sanhedrin, Maimonides provides a lengthy discussion of forbidden unions, bestiality, lesbianism, homosexuality and other matters pertaining to sex ethics. This *Mishnah* and Maimonides' commentary thereto are presented below, the latter translated for the first time into English from the recent Hebrew and Arabic edition of Rabbi Joseph Kapach (Jerusalem: Mossad Harav Kook, 1965, pp. 175–184).

Excerpts from Maimonides' *Commentary on the Mishnah*

Sanhedrin, Chapter 7, Mishnah 4

These are they that are to be stoned: he that has sexual intercourse with his mother, with the wife of his father, with his daughter-in-law, with a male, or with a beast, and the woman who copulates with a beast, the blasphemer, the idolater, he who offers of his seed to *Molech,*[1] he given to necromancy and the soothsayer, he who profanes the Sabbath, he that curses his father or his mother, he that has sexual connection with a betrothed maiden, he who entices (others to idolatry), he that misleads (a whole town to idolatry), the sorcerer, and the rebellious and disobedient son.[2] He that has intercourse with his mother is thereby liable[3] because of "(the law of) the mother" and because of "(the law of) the father's wife."[4] R. Judah says, he is only culpable according to "(the law of) the mother." He who has connection with his father's wife is thereby liable because of "(the law of) the father's wife" and because of "(the law of) another man's wife,"[5] whether during the lifetime of his father or after the death of his father, whether following betrothal or after marriage. He who has sexual connection with his daughter-in-law is thereby guilty because of "(the law of) one's daughter-in-law[6] and because of "(the law of) another man's wife," whether in the lifetime of his son or after his son's death, whether after the betrothal or after wedlock. He that has connection with a male or with a beast, and the woman that has connection with a beast (are to be stoned).[7] If the man has sinned, how has the beast sinned? Because an offense has befallen a man through it, therefore Scripture has said that it must be stoned; another reason (why it must be stoned) is that lest the animal pass through the street and they say, "This is it because of which so-and-so was stoned."

Maimonides' Commentary

Wherever the Torah uses the expression *"their blood is upon them,"*[8] the punishment referred to is stoning. Stoning for one who lies with a beast is derived from the phrase *"he shall surely be put to death,"*[9] and from *"and the beast ye shall also slay."*[10] Concerning one who incites individuals to idolatry, it is written *"thou shalt surely kill him"*;[11] just as the inciter is stoned, so too the animal; and the same death that is inflicted upon the animal is meted out to the person that lies with it.[12] It is well known that one who causes another man to have sexual connection with him is stoned, and this is called *nirvah lezachor.* Similarly a person who carnally brings an animal upon himself is stoned, and this is called *nirvah lebehemah.*[13] These acts are included in the prohibition of *"whosoever lieth with a beast, etc."*[14] The same applies to a woman who causes herself to be bestially abused whether naturally or unnaturally. The same also applies to a man who commits bestiality, whether naturally or unnaturally.[15]

This seems to be an appropriate place for me to mention extremely important principles concerning forbidden unions. Although these principles are scattered in many places throughout the *Mishnah,* and we have explained each principle in its place, I will gather them all together here in order that they should all be found in one place for anyone wishing to delve into them. I will also mention matters which are not explained in the *Mishnah* so that the entire subject will be complete.

Let me begin by saying that whatever I say about an adult man refers to a male who is thirteen years and one day old who has two pubic hairs (as a sign of puberty), for this is the definition of a man in our Torah. Similarly a girl of twelve years and one day who has two pubic hairs is called an adult. Anyone less than these ages, or one who has reached such an age but has not shown evidence of two pubic hairs is called a minor. Wherever I say that a person is worthy of being punished, I refer to flogging, or one of the court-imposed death penalties.

After making these introductory remarks, I will begin with a discussion of the principles which I promised to mention here. Let me say that concerning all the forbidden unions, there is no difference whether the sexual intercourse is performed naturally or unnaturally.[16] Natural intercourse is when the man faces his partner, and unnatural intercourse refers to posterior penetration. There is also no difference regarding an initiator *(me'areh)* or a consummator *(Gomer)* *(vide infra)* as to whether they perform sexual intercourse naturally or unnaturally.[17] The same is true of an initiator of pederasty and an initiator of bestiality.[18] An initiator is one who inserts the entire glans penis, whereas a consummator is one who inserts the entire penis. The insertion of only part of the glans is equivalent to one who has carnal contact of sexual organs (without actual penetration). The emission of semen has no relationship at all to the matter of the punishment. Therefore, as soon as he inserts his organ, he incurs the punishment, even if he withdrew immediately. There is also no difference in all the forbidden unions whether the man is above and the woman below, or whether the man is below and the woman is above. The latter is called reversed coitus.[19] The same applies to all other positions of intercourse, that is, the perpetrators become culpable and incur punishment with the insertion of the glans, no matter what position they are in.

And if a man had sexual intercourse with any one of the forbidden unions without having an erection, he does not incur punishment, even if he emitted semen, because there is difference of opinion on this question, and the Talmud does not provide the final ruling; and one does not inflict punishment save in a matter which is clear, and about which there is no doubt. However, such an act is (still strictly) forbidden and this is what the Sages have called having intercourse with a dead organ,[20] meaning his organ is flaccid like a corpse. However, everyone agrees that he who has sexual intercourse with a deceased forbidden relative does not incur any punishment at all,[21] and this is called an act of Herod.[22]

Whosoever has intercourse with a woman of the forbidden unions, whether by way of carnal contact of sexual organs (without actual penetration) or by kissing her or by embracing or touching one of her organs, thus deriving pleasure therefrom—no matter which organ (or limb) of her body that he touches in the manner that some people derive pleasure from touching with their hand or their foot—is called by the Sages as fornicator with hand and foot,[23] and such action portrays a picture of abomination. Similarly, to jest or act frivolously with a woman of the forbidden unions or to wink at her for the sake of deriving pleasure is all prohibited. He who does these things incurs flogging. All these acts are included in two negative commandments mentioned in the *Torah.* The first is *none of you shall approach to any that is near of kin to him to uncover their nakedness*[24] which means to say you should remain distant from things which lead to and accustom one to forbidden unions. And so, too, do the Sages explain it: do not approach and then you will not uncover their nakedness. The second (Biblical prohibition) is that *ye do not any of these abominable customs,*[25] and the aforementioned actions and the like are called abominable customs. However, a person only incurs Heavenly death *(Kareth)* for sexual intercourse, as previously explained and as the Sages stated: for the abominations themselves the penalty is Heavenly death.[26]

And it is forbidden to even smell her perfume or to satiate one's eye by gazing at her beauty with the intent of deriving pleasure therefrom. However, no flogging is incurred for these acts. Even though the Sages interpreted the phrase *lo tinaf*[27] to mean *lo tehaneh le'af,*[28] no flogging is given for this act.[29]

It is permissible to gaze at a bride at her wedding,[30] even though she is a married woman and one of the forbidden unions. It is prohibited to gaze at her afterwards, except if he had no intention of viewing her figure. An unmarried woman may be gazed upon by a man who is not forbidden to her, even if he derived pleasure from beholding her figure. There is no prohibition in such an act. However, because of modesty, one should refrain from this permissible act in order not to be entrapped in a forbidden act. The pious abhor this practice (of gazing at a virgin) even though it is permissible. They are concerned lest that woman become married, and he will continue to gaze at her because he has become accustomed to do so. The Sages explicitly interpreted the words of Job in this manner: *I made a covenant with mine eyes, how then should I look upon a maiden?*[31] However, it is not prohibited.

However, if he gazes at her to see whether she is beautiful so that he might marry her, or to see whether she has an ugly figure in which case he would not marry her, this is an obligation,[32] and the Torah encourages him to do so. Even modest people who are strict Torah observers do this.

One who has sexual intercourse with an unmarried woman incurs flogging, and the woman does not become ineligible to marry a priest, nor is she called a prostitute. However, one who has carnal contact of sexual organs (without actual penetration) with an unmarried woman, and one who performs any of the other acts (such as kissing and embracing) which we previously stated would make the perpetrator incur flogging, if committed with one of the forbidden unions, does not get flogged. For only actual sexual intercourse with an unmarried woman requires flogging (as a penalty), as we have explained. However, all the other acts are also prohibited, and are not permissible at all.

Flogging is meted out by Rabbinic decree for a person who secludes himself with an unmarried woman.[33] Similarly a person is forbidden to seclude himself with any woman of the forbidden unions. The only exceptions are seclusion with another man or with an animal, for the Sages said that Israelites are not under suspicion of sodomy with males or of bestiality.[34] For this pure people does not lust for these two acts which are totally unnatural. Therefore, if a man secludes himself with one of the women of the forbidden unions, with whom he is forbidden to be secluded, or with an unmarried woman who is not among the forbidden unions, they should both be flogged. The only exception is a married woman; although it is forbidden to be secluded with her, nevertheless, if a man secluded himself with her, they are not flogged, neither she nor he, in order not to stigmatize her children as bastards.

A person is only permitted to seclude himself with his mother or his daughter. It is prohibited for a person to seclude himself with any other woman of the forbidden unions. We have already explained all the laws of seclusion at the end of *Kiddushin.*[35]

Although the nature of Torah-observant individuals is not to become aroused or derive pleasure from kissing female relatives, such as one's sister or maternal aunt or paternal aunt or granddaughter, such an act is most disgraceful and is forbidden. There is no penalty of flogging incurred if there was no intent of deriving pleasure; nevertheless, it is still prohibited. One of the Sages of blessed memory used to kiss the bosom or the hand of his older sister when he returned from the house of learning, but then he refrained from this and carefully avoided such acts when he realized that this is not permissible.[36] And the Sages stated "Go, go, thou Nazarite, take the most devious route, but approach not the vineyard."[37] The sole exceptions in this matter are a mother with a son and a father with his daughter, in that a mother is permitted to kiss her son and to embrace him until he becomes twelve years old, at which time he becomes prohibited to her like all other forbidden unions. Similarly, a father is permitted to kiss his daughter and to embrace her until she becomes nine years old and then she is prohibited to him.[38]

It is prohibited for a woman to serve a man, such as to pour his beverage or serve his food or wash his hands or the like, whether she is an adult in years (i.e., twelve years and one day) or only three years and one day old, whether she is a free woman or a bondswoman, whether she is pubertal or prepubertal, whether she is a virgin or deflorated, whether she is one of the forbidden unions to him or not. The only exceptions are the mother and the daughter, as we mentioned previously, irrespective of their age. The Sages said that one should not make use of a woman at all,[39] the reason being that a man not come to sinful thoughts. However, flogging is not incurred therefore. The Sages strongly warned against licentious thoughts and things that provoke them. They spoke at length that a person should fear and be afraid of intentionally producing an erection[40] and of emitting semen for naught[41] and they explained that all such acts are prohibited. However, they did not impose flogging as a penalty for any of these.

Similarly, the abominable practice of lesbianism between women who lie one with the other is a disgraceful practice. However, there is no punishment therefore, either Biblical or Rabbinic. None of such women is called a prostitute, and none is prohibited to her husband. Nor is such a woman forbidden for the priesthood. These are women which the Sages have called *mesoleloth* (lesbians), from the word *maslol,* which is the manner of practicing lewdness one with the other.[42] Although there is no punishment for this act, the Sages consider it among the abominations of Egypt as they explicitly stated (in their interpretation of the phrase) *the doings of the land of Egypt.*[43] "What did they do? A man would marry a man, or a woman would marry a woman, or a woman would marry two men."[44]

It is permissible for a man to have intercourse with his wife unnaturally or by carnal contact (without actual penetration) or in any manner he wishes. Thus, too, was the reply of the Sages to a woman who inquired about this. They said: The Torah has permitted it.[45] One of the Sages tried to establish that it is shameful for a man to have intercourse with his wife in the aforementioned manners, or to have intercourse with her in the fashions of the multitude of people who have a great deal of lust, such as the reverse position (i.e., the woman on top) or the kissing of the private parts of the body and the like. The other Sages, however, argue with him and affirm that a man is permitted to act with his wife in any fashion he wishes, and the final ruling in the Talmud is according to these Sages. Although all the above is permissible, as we have mentioned, pious and modest people refrain from such animalistic behavior and consider it disgraceful. They also consider debased those who direct their thoughts and lusts to these acts.

For since the true design of intercourse is to propagate the race and not only for sexual pleasure, then the pleasurable part of coitus was only given to stimulate human beings towards the major goal of the sexual act which is to maintain the seed (of humanity). Clear evidence for this contention is the fact that lust ceases and sensual delight subsides after the emission of the semen, because for this purpose (of producing progeny) alone is the nature of man aroused. For if the goal were only sexual enjoyment, then a person should be able to have sexual gratification whenever he desired it, but the fact of the matter is not so. Therefore, the goal of the pious is only to satisfy the goal of nature, and the Sages praise and cherish such an attitude and call such a person one who "sanctifies himself during intercourse,"[46] that is, he conducts himself only in a permissible (i.e., modest) manner. They further stated that such conduct imparts to the offspring purity and modesty and excellence of character.

The Sages greatly praised one of the scholars whose wife had blemishes which were readily apparent and visible, yet he did not perceive it,[47] for his mind was occupied with that which pious and pure people are occupied, that is, when he had intercourse with her (he was modest and did not scrutinize her, but) his goal was purely the goal of nature in Godly wisdom. This does not contradict our previous statement when we mentioned that a person is permitted to behave with his wife in any manner he wishes. For exclusive of prohibited versus permissible behavior are abominable and detestable versus desirable and praiseworthy behavior. One should strive for modesty and extreme self-restraint.

The Sages also prohibited a man from having intercourse with his wife by the light of a lamp,[48] but there is no penalty incurred therefore. They also prohibited a man from having intercourse with his wife in public places or in gardens and orchards,[49] and other sites which are not dwelling places. They inflict disciplinary (as opposed to judicial) flogging for such behavior. The Sages also consider detestable intercourse during daylight,[50] and excessive intercourse with his wife,[51] and with too many wives, and marriage to the daughter of an ignoramus, or the taking of an ignoramus as a groom,[52] and marriage to a girl who is less than twelve years old,[53] and the marriage of a young girl to an old man, or an old woman to a young boy. All these actions constitute shameless behavior according to our Torah.[54]

I will now return to the principles which we began to explain and (try to) complete them. If an adult man fornicated with a minor—if she is three years and one day old or older—he incurs a punishment, but she incurs no penalty unless she was an adult.[55] If an adult woman fornicated with a young boy—if he is nine years and one day old or older—she incurs a punishment, but he incurs no penalty unless he was an adult.[56]

If an adult man who has sexual intercourse with another male or allows a male to practice sodomy with him is nine years and one day old or older, the man is killed, and the male partner is not killed unless he, too, is an adult. And if a woman who copulates with an animal is three years and one day old or older, the animal is killed, but she is not killed unless she is an adult. If she is less than three years and one day old, even the animal is not killed. Similarly, if a man who copulates with an animal or allows an animal to copulate with him is nine years and one day old or older, the animal is killed; and he does not incur the death penalty unless he is an adult. One pays no attention to the age of the animal, and an adult and a young beast are considered equal. Also (equally prohibited is) active or passive bestiality and it also matters not whether the animal is male or female.[57]

The sexual intercourse of any boy below age nine years and one day is not considered valid, and it is as if he did nothing insofar as the punishment is concerned. However, it is absolutely prohibited. Whether he is the active or the passive partner, there is no penalty incurred as a result of his intercourse. Similarly the sexual intercourse of a girl less than three years and one day old is not considered valid, whether she copulates with a man or with a beast.

You should also know that a woman who commits bestiality with an animal is not prohibited to her husband even if he is a priest.[58] We have already explained that the courts punish an adult man and an adult woman on the testimony of witnesses and after proper warning (for such a crime); all this has already been explained. But if the courts do not know (of such a crime) and do not inflict punishment, or if the testimony (of witnesses) is not upheld, know that the sin of the perpetrators is written before the Almighty, and He will punish the sinner according to the deed and according to His justice. We know from tradition that the Holy One Blessed be He does not inflict *kareth* (premature death) except after age twenty-one years,[59] and there is no difference in this matter between males and females.

You should also know that the wife of a man who is not an adult is not considered a (fully) married woman.[60] The same applies to the wife of a deaf-mute or an imbecile if she married him when he already was a deaf-mute or an imbecile.[61] However, if the father betrothed his minor daughter or his adult deaf-mute daughter to a man, she is considered a fully married woman. But a deaf-mute woman or an imbecile who married herself is not considered a fully married woman, either in regard to the death penalty or in regard to bringing an offering (in the time of the Temple).

Know also that if a man had sexual intercourse with a woman and with her mother, or with two sisters, or two other relatives, it is as if he had intercourse with two unrelated women. For the forbidden relatives mentioned in the Torah only apply if one of them was his own wife. He is permitted to marry any of them after he has fornicated with her, according to the conditions that we explained in the eleventh chapter of *Yebamoth.*[62] And if a man has intercourse with a relative of his wife, such as her mother or her sister or her daughter or the like, his wife does not become prohibited to him, even though he incurs (Divine) *kareth*, or death (by the courts). However, if a woman voluntarily prostituted with another man, she becomes prohibited to her husband, even if she had intercourse with a Gentile. If she was raped, she remains permitted to her husband, unless he is a priest.

This is what I thought appropriate to mention here concerning forbidden unions and other similar prohibited intercourses, and that which is abominable and forbidden and despicable, and that which is praiseworthy.

And the final ruling (in this *Mishnah*) is not like Rabbi Judah.

Notes

1. The god of fire and an idol of the Canaanites and Ammonites and others to which the idolatrous Israelites offered human sacrifices.
2. Deut. 21, 18 et. seq.
3. To two *sin-offerings* if the offense was committed unwittingly. Levit. 4, 27.
4. Levit. 18, 7, 8.
5. Levit. 18, 20.
6. Levit. 18, 15.
7. Levit. 20, 15, 16; Niddah 36b; Baba Bathra 1:4; Sanhedrin 54b.
8. Levit. 20: 11, 12, 13, 16, 27.
9. Exod. 22:18.
10. Levit. 20:15.
11. Deut. 13:10.
12. Sanhedrin 54b.
13. *Ibid.*
14. Exod. 22:18.
15. Sanhedrin 55a.
16. *Ibid.* 54a.
17. Yebamoth 6:1 and 54b to 55a.

18. Sanhedrin 55a.
19. See Nedarim 20a and Rashi there.
20. Sanhedrin 55a; Yebamoth 95b; Shebuoth 18a.
21. Yebamoth 55b.
22. Herod set his eyes on a certain maiden but she committed suicide. Herod preserved her body in honey for seven years and (some say) had sexual intercourse with her (Baba Bathra 3b).
23. Niddah 13b.
24. Levit. 18:6.
25. Levit. 18:30.
26. Levit. 18:30.
27. *Thou shalt not commit adultery.*
28. Do not derive pleasure with the nose, i.e., by smelling her perfume.
29. Jerusalem Talmud. Berachoth 8:6
30. lit.: at the time of the blessing.
31. Job 31:1.
32. Kiddushin 41a.
33. Kiddushin 81a.
34. *Ibid* 82a.
35. Chapter 4, Mishnah 12.
36. Shabbath 13a.
37. Pesachim 40b; Yebamoth 46a; Baba Metzia 92a; Avodah Zarah 17a, 58b and 59a.
38. Kiddushin 81b.
39. Kiddushin 70a and 81b.
40. Niddah 13b.
41. *Ibid.* 13a.
42. Yebamoth 76a.
43. Levit. 18:3.
44. Sifra on Levit. 18:3.
45. Nedarim 20b.
46. Shebuoth 18b.
47. Shabbath 53b.
48. Betzah 22a.
49. Yebamoth 90b and Sanhedrin 46a.
50. Niddah 17a.
51. Berachoth 22a.
52. Pesachim 49b.

53. Niddah 13b.
54. Sanhedrin 86b and Yebamoth 106b.
55. Yebamoth 57b; Kiddushin 10a; Niddah 44b.
56. Sanhedrin 55b; Baba Bathra 156a; Niddah 54a.
57. Sanhedrin 54b and 55a.
58. Yebamoth 59b.
59. Shabbath 89b.
60. Kiddushin 50b.
61. Yebamoth 112b.
62. Mishnah 1.

Index

abortion, 76
adolescence, 70
adultery, 85, 88, 92, 94, 106
Al Afdal Nur ad Din Ali, 4, 45, 58
Al Fadhil, 7
Al Farabi, 4
Al Mutsaffar ben Ajjub, ix
Aldabi, Meir, 13–14
Alfadhal, Vizier, 4
Alharizi, Jehudah, 78
aphrodisiacs, 17–29, 74–75
apoplexy, 67
Aristotle, 4, 83
arthritis, 51
Asher ben Yechiel, Rabbi, 14
asthma, 52–53
Avenzoar, 4, 13
Avicenna, 13, 24

bastardy, 92, 97
bestiality, 86, 94, 98, 112, 113–14, 115, 118, 122, 123
black bile, 71, 75
blood, 70–71
Book of Commandments (Maimonides), 6
Book of Holiness (Maimonides), 93–109
Book on Logic (Maimonides), 6
Book of Women (Maimonides), 110–11

castration, 77, 97
chastity, 95, 97, 108–109
childbirth, 70, 71
cervix uteri, 71, 76
circumcision, 89–92
cleanliness, 62–63, 82–83
clubbing, 68
Code of Maimonides. See *Mishneh Torah*
Commentary on the Aphorisms of Hippocrates (Maimonides), 49–51

Commentary on the Mishnah (Maimonides), 6, 112–26
corpus uteri, 71

diabetes, 67
Discourse on the Explanation of Fits (Maimonides), 58–60
divorce, 85, 92, 97, 106, 110

emphysema, 67–68
Epistle to Yemen (Maimonides), 6
eunuchs, 97, 105, 110
Extracts from Galen (Maimonides), 6–7, 13

fetus, 70, 71
flatulence, 21, 71, 73

Galen, 4, 6–7, 45, 49, 51, 55
genitalia, 70, 71, 75, 76
Glossary of Drug Names (Maimonides), 8
Guide for the Perplexed (Maimonides), 6, 78–92

hemorrhoids, 42–44
hepatitis, 68
hermaphrodites, 98, 110
Hertz, J. H., 93
Hippocrates, 4, 45, 49–51, 55
homosexuality, 94, 97–98, 112
Ibn Tibbon, Samuel, 4, 78
Ibn Yitzchak, Hunain, 49
Ibn Zohr, 4, 27

Laws of Temperament (Maimonides), 62–65
lesbianism, 94, 101, 112, 119–20

Maimonides, Moses
  Book of Commandments, 6
  Book of Holiness, 93–109
  Book on Logic, 6
  Book of Women, 110–11
  Code. See *Mishneh Torah*
  Commentary on the Aphorisms of Hippocrates, 49–51
  Commentary on the Mishnah, 6, 112–26
  Discourse on the Explanation of Fits, 58–60
  Epistle to Yemen, 6
  Extracts from Galen, 6–7, 13
  Glossary of Drug Names, 8
  Guide for the Perplexed, 6, 78–92
  Laws of Temperament, 62–65
  Medical Answers, 58–60
  Medical Aphorisms of Moses Maimonides, 9, 66–77
  Mishneh Torah, 6, 61–65, 80, 81, 94
  Regimen of Health, 9, 45–48, 58
  Treatise on Asthma, 52–57

Index

Treatise on Cohabitation, ix, 11–40
Treatise on Hemorrhoids, 42–44
Treatise on Poisons and Their Antidotes, 7–8, 9
Treatise on Resurrection, 6
marriage, 84–88, 93–95, 96–97, 106, 110, 111, 123
masturbation, 77, 94, 104
Medical Answers (Maimonides), 58–60
Medical Aphorisms of Moses Maimonides, 9, 66–77
melancholia, 72
menstruation, 19, 88, 94, 97, 100
Mishneh Torah, (Maimonides), 6, 61–65, 80, 81, 94
Moses ben Samuel Ibn Tibbon, 46, 49

onanism, 94, 104
Osler, Sir William, 9
ovaries, 76–77

pederasty, 86, 115
pneumonia, 68
poisons, 7–8, 9
Prayer of Maimonides, 6
pregnancy, 70, 71, 76
prohibitions, sexual, 86–88, 93–109, 112–124
prostitution, 81, 84, 92, 97, 101, 111
puberty, 19, 76, 110

rape, 94, 110, 124
Regimen of Health (Maimonides), 9, 45–48, 58
Rhazes of Persia, 4
Richard the Lion-Hearted, 4

Saladin the Great, 4
semen, 18, 69–70, 70–71, 72, 73–74, 75
Sheviley Emunah (Aldabi), 14
sodomy, 94, 118, 122
stroke, 67

Treatise on Asthma (Maimonides), 52–57
Treatise on Cohabitation (Maimonides), ix, 11–40
Treatise on Hemorrhoids (Maimonides), 42–44
Treatise on Poisons and Their Antidotes (Maimonides), 7–8, 9
Treatise on Resurrection (Maimonides), 6

uterus, 70, 71, 75, 76

virginity, 110, 111

widows, marriage to, 92, 97

About the Author

Fred Rosner, M.D., F.A.C.P., is director of the Department of Medicine of the Mount Sinai Services at the Queens Hospital Center and professor of medicine at New York's Mount Sinai School of Medicine. He is a diplomate of the American Board of Internal Medicine, a fellow of the American College of Physicians, and the recipient of numerous awards.

Dr. Rosner is an internationally known authority on medical ethics. He has lectured widely on Jewish medical ethics and is in great demand as a speaker on this and related topics. He has served as a visiting professor or lecturer in England, France, Germany, Mexico, Canada, Holland, Israel, South Africa, and throughout the United States. He is a member of the Professional Advisory Board of the prestigious Kennedy Institute for Ethics of Georgetown University, as well as chairman of the Medical Ethics Committee of the Medical Society of the State of New York.

He is the author of five widely acclaimed books on Jewish medical ethics, including *Modern Medicine and Jewish Ethics* and the two-volume *Medicine and Jewish Law*. These books are up-to-date examinations of the Jewish view on many important bioethical issues in medical practice. A noted Maimonidean scholar, Dr. Rosner has translated and published, in English, most of Maimonides' medical writings.